TABLE OF CONTEN

Top 20 Test Taking Tips 4

Overview 5

Classification of Drugs 39

Pharmacological Principles 53

Alcohol and Tobacco 70

Sedative Hypnotics 88

Stimulants 100

Opioids 109

Hallucinogens 113

Other Drugs 123

Prevention/Treatment 136

Practice Test 155

    Practice Questions 155

    Answers and Explanations 158

Secret Key #1 - Time is Your Greatest Enemy 161

    Pace Yourself 161

Secret Key #2 - Guessing is not Guesswork 162

    Monkeys Take the Test 162

    $5 Challenge 163

Secret Key #3 - Practice Smarter, Not Harder 164

    Success Strategy 164

Secret Key #4 - Prepare, Don't Procrastinate 165

Secret Key #5 - Test Yourself 166

General Strategies 167

Special Report: Additional Bonus Material 175

Top 20 Test Taking Tips

1. Carefully follow all the test registration procedures
2. Know the test directions, duration, topics, question types, how many questions
3. Setup a flexible study schedule at least 3-4 weeks before test day
4. Study during the time of day you are most alert, relaxed, and stress free
5. Maximize your learning style; visual learner use visual study aids, auditory learner use auditory study aids
6. Focus on your weakest knowledge base
7. Find a study partner to review with and help clarify questions
8. Practice, practice, practice
9. Get a good night's sleep; don't try to cram the night before the test
10. Eat a well balanced meal
11. Know the exact physical location of the testing site; drive the route to the site prior to test day
12. Bring a set of ear plugs; the testing center could be noisy
13. Wear comfortable, loose fitting, layered clothing to the testing center; prepare for it to be either cold or hot during the test
14. Bring at least 2 current forms of ID to the testing center
15. Arrive to the test early; be prepared to wait and be patient
16. Eliminate the obviously wrong answer choices, then guess the first remaining choice
17. Pace yourself; don't rush, but keep working and move on if you get stuck
18. Maintain a positive attitude even if the test is going poorly
19. Keep your first answer unless you are positive it is wrong
20. Check your work, don't make a careless mistake

Overview

WHO definitions

1964 definition of drug dependence

Various attempts have been made to find a term that could be applied to drug abuse generally—a particularly troublesome endeavor. The component in common appears to be dependence, whether psychic or physical or both. Hence, use of the term 'drug dependence', with a modifying phase linking it to a particular drug type in order to differentiate one class of drugs from another, had been given most careful consideration. The Committee recommends substitution of the term 'drug dependence' for the terms 'drug addiction' and 'drug habituation'. The committee did not clearly define dependence, but did go on to clarify that there was a distinction between physical and psychological dependence. It said that drug abuse was "a state of psychic dependence or physical dependence, or both, on a drug, arising in a person following administration of that drug on a periodic or continued basis." Psychic dependence was defined as a state in which "there is a feeling of satisfaction and psychic drive that requires periodic or continuous administration of the drug to produce pleasure or to avoid discomfort." There is scarcely any agent that can be taken into the body to which some individuals will not get a reaction satisfactory or pleasurable to them, persuading them to continue its use even to the point of abuse — that is, to excessive or persistent use beyond medical need.

Drug addiction and drug habituation

The 1957 World Health Organization (WHO) Expert Committee on Addiction-Producing Drugs defined addiction and habituation as components of drug abuse: Drug addiction is a state of periodic or chronic intoxication produced by the repeated consumption of a drug (natural or synthetic). Its characteristics include: (i) an overpowering desire or need (compulsion) to continue taking the drug and to obtain it by any means; (ii) a tendency to increase the dose; (iii) a psychic (psychological) and generally a physical dependence on the effects of the drug; and (iv) detrimental effects on the individual and on society.

Drug habituation (habit) is a condition resulting from the repeated consumption of a drug. Its characteristics include (i) a desire (but not a compulsion) to continue taking the drug for the sense of improved well-being which it engenders; (ii) little or no tendency to increase the dose; (iii) some degree of psychic dependence on the effect of the drug, but absence of physical dependence and hence of an abstinence syndrome [withdrawal], and (iv) detrimental effects, if any, primarily on the individual.

The definitions of addiction, physical dependence, tolerance and pseudoaddiction according to the 2001 American Academy of Pain Medicine, American Pain Society, and American Society of Addiction Medicine who jointly issued "Definitions Related to the Use of Opioids for the Treatment of Pain."

Addiction is a primary, chronic, neurobiologic disease, with genetic, psychosocial, and environmental factors influencing its development and manifestations. It is characterized by behaviors that include one or more of the following: impaired control over drug use, compulsive use, continued use despite harm, and craving. Physical dependence is a state of adaptation that is manifested by a drug class specific withdrawal syndrome that can be produced by abrupt cessation, rapid dose reduction, decreasing blood level of the drug, and/or administration of an antagonist.

Tolerance is the body's physical adaptation to a drug: greater amounts of the drug are required over time to achieve the initial effect as the body "gets used to" and adapts to the intake.

Pseudoaddiction is a term which has been used to describe patient behaviors that may occur when pain is undertreated. Patients with unrelieved pain may become focused on obtaining medications, may "clock watch," and may otherwise seem inappropriately "drug seeking." Even such behaviors as illicit drug use and deception can occur in the patient's efforts to obtain relief. Pseudoaddiction can be distinguished from true addiction in that the behaviors resolve when pain is effectively treated.

Drug abuse

A drug is any chemical substance that changes the way a person acts or feels. Drugs may affect a person's mental, physical, or emotional state. Though many drugs are taken to improve the condition of the body or to remedy personal problems, drugs can also undermine health by distorting a person's mind and weakening a person's body. According to the World Health Organization, drug abuse is any excessive drug use that is not approved by the medical profession. The use of some drugs in any quantity is considered abuse; other drugs must be taken in large quantities before they are considered to have been abused. There are health risks involved with the use of any drug, legal or illegal, insofar as they introduce a foreign substance into the balanced system of physical health.

Substance abuse refers to the overindulgence in and dependence upon a drug or other chemical leading to effects that are detrimental to the individual's physical and mental health, or the welfare of others. The disorder is characterized by a pattern of continued pathological use of a medication, non-medically indicated drug or toxin, that results in repeated adverse social consequences related to drug use, such as failure to meet work, family, or school obligations, interpersonal conflicts, or legal problems. There are on-going debates as to the exact distinctions between substance abuse and substance dependence, but current practice standard distinguishes between the two by defining substance dependence in terms of physiological and behavioral symptoms of substance use, and substance abuse in terms of the social consequences of substance use. Substance abuse may lead to addiction or substance dependence. Medically, physiological dependence requires the development of tolerance leading to withdrawal symptoms. Both abuse and dependence are distinct from addiction which involves a compulsion to continue using the substance despite the negative consequences, and may or may not involve chemical dependency. Dependence almost always implies abuse, but abuse frequently occurs without dependence, particularly when an individual first begins to abuse a substance. Dependence involves physiological processes while substance abuse reflects a complex interaction between the individual, the abused substance and society.

Depending on the actual compound, drug abuse may lead to health problems, social problems, physical dependence, or psychological addiction. Some drugs that are subject to abuse have central nervous system (CNS) effects, which produce changes in mood, levels of awareness or perceptions and sensations. Most of these drugs also alter systems other than the CNS. But, not all centrally acting drugs are subject to abuse, which suggests that altering consciousness is not sufficient for a drug to have abuse potential. Among drugs that are abused, some appear to be more likely to lead to uncontrolled use than others, suggesting a possible hierarchy of drug-induced effects relative to abuse potential.

In the early 1950s, the first edition of the American Psychiatric Association's Diagnostic and Statistical Manual of Mental Disorders referred to both alcohol and drug abuse as part of Sociopathic Personality Disturbances, which were thought to be symptoms of deeper psychological disorders or moral weakness. By the third edition, in the 1980s, drug abuse was grouped into 'substance abuse'. In 1972, the American Psychiatric Association created a definition that used legality, social acceptability, and even cultural familiarity as qualifying factors:

...as a general rule, we reserve the term drug abuse to apply to the illegal, non-medical use of a limited number of substances, most of them drugs, which have properties of altering the mental state in ways that are considered by social norms and defined by statute to be inappropriate, undesirable, harmful, threatening, or, at minimum, culture-alien.

In 1966, the American Medical Association's Committee on Alcoholism and Addiction defined abuse of stimulants (amphetamines, primarily) in terms of "medical supervision":

..."use" refers to the proper place of stimulants in medical practice; "misuse" applies to the physician's role in initiating a potentially dangerous course of therapy; and "abuse" refers to self-administration of these drugs without medical supervision and particularly in large doses that may lead to psychological dependency, tolerance and abnormal behavior.

In the modern medical profession, the two most used diagnostic tools in the world, the American Psychiatric Association's Diagnostic and Statistical Manual of Mental Disorders (DSM) and the World Health Organization's International Statistical Classification of Diseases and Related Health Problems (ICD), no longer recognize 'drug abuse' as a current medical diagnosis. Instead, they have adopted substance abuse as a blanket term to include drug abuse and other things. However, other definitions differ; they may entail psychological or physical dependence, and may focus on treatment and prevention in terms of the social consequences of substance uses.

In the early 1950s, the first edition of the American Psychiatric Association's Diagnostic and Statistical Manual of Mental Disorders grouped alcohol and drug abuse under Sociopathic Personality Disturbances, which were thought to be symptoms of deeper psychological disorders or moral weakness. The third edition, in the 1980s, was the first to recognize substance abuse (including drug abuse) and substance dependence as conditions separate from substance abuse alone, bringing in social and cultural factors. The definition of dependence emphasized tolerance to drugs, and withdrawal from them as key components to diagnosis, whereas abuse was defined as "problematic use with social or occupational impairment" but without withdrawal or tolerance.

In 1987 the DSM-IIIR category "psychoactive substance abuse", which includes former concepts of drug abuse is defined as "a maladaptive pattern of use indicated by...continued use despite knowledge of having a persistent or recurrent social, occupational, psychological or physical problem that is caused or exacerbated by the use (or by) recurrent use in situations in which it is physically hazardous. It is a residual category, with dependence taking precedence when applicable. It was the first definition to give equal weight to behavioral and physiological factors in diagnosis.

By 1988, the DSM-III-R had defined substance dependence as "a syndrome involving compulsive use, with or without tolerance and withdrawal"; whereas substance abuse is "problematic use without compulsive use, significant tolerance, or withdrawal". By 1994, the fourth edition of the Diagnostic and Statistical Manual of Mental Disorders (DSM-IV) issued by the American Psychiatric Association defined substance abuse as:

- A maladaptive pattern of substance use leading to clinically significant impairment or distress, as manifested by one (or more) of the following, occurring within a 12-month period:
    - Recurrent substance use resulting in a failure to fulfill major role obligations at work, school, or home (e.g., repeated absences or poor work performance related to substance use)
    - Recurrent substance use in situations in which it is physically hazardous (e.g., driving an automobile or operating a machine when impaired by substance use)

- o Recurrent substance-related legal problems (e.g., arrests for substance-related disorderly conduct)
- o Continued substance use despite having persistent or recurrent social or interpersonal problems caused or exacerbated by the effects of the substance (e.g., arguments with spouse about consequences of intoxication, physical fights)
- The symptoms have never met the criteria for Substance Dependence for this class of substance.

Reasons for adult drug abuse

Although adults are supposed to be more mature than teenagers and do the right things, there are still those who abuse drugs. Adult drug abuse includes several different types of drugs, including marijuana and methamphetamines. Some parents feel that it is okay to abuse narcotics with their children. They think that marijuana is a harmless drug and feel that sharing a joint with their teens every once in a while will make them more like friends. Additionally, some baby boomers who are now parents have never given up using drugs and do not have a problem with their children using drugs. Some of these parents buy the drugs for their children.

In 1998, methamphetamines were ranked 9th out of all drug-related deaths, with 501 methamphetamine-related deaths, accounting for 5% of to total drug-related deaths. 208 of the deaths were males who were 35 years of age or older. 31% of methamphetamine-related emergency room attendees who were treated in 1998 were 35 and older.

Elderly people are not known for using abusing drugs. If they are abusing drugs most likely they are abusing prescribed psychoactive drugs to solve their problems with insomnia, anxiety, and depression. Older people are less likely to use street drugs such as heroin, cocaine or marijuana. It is not known if this is because of their body changes and the affects these have on the way they get their highs or if they simply do not want to deal with the hassles of that which comes along with doing these drugs.

Drug addiction

Addiction is the repeated use of a psychoactive substance or substances to the extent that the user (referred to as an addict) is periodically or chronically intoxicated, shows a compulsion to take the preferred substance (or substances), has great difficulty in voluntarily ceasing or modifying substance use, and exhibits determination to obtain psychoactive substances by almost any means. Typically, tolerance is prominent and a withdrawal syndrome frequently occurs when substance use is interrupted. The life of the addict may be dominated by substance use to the virtual exclusion of all other activities and responsibilities. The term addiction also conveys the sense that such substance use has a detrimental effect on society, as well as on the individual; when applied to the use of alcohol, it is equivalent to alcoholism. Addiction is a term of long-standing and variable usage. It is regarded by many as a discrete disease entity, a debilitating disorder rooted in the pharmacological effects of the drug, which is remorselessly progressive. From the 1920s to the 1960s attempts were made to differentiate between addiction and "habituation", a less severe form of psychological adaptation. In the 1960s the World Health Organization recommended that both terms be abandoned in favor of dependence, which can exist in various degrees of severity. Addiction is not a diagnostic term in ICD-10, but continues to be very widely employed by professionals and the general public alike.

Drug addiction is considered a pathological state. The disorder of addiction involves the progression of acute drug use to the development of drug-seeking behavior, the vulnerability to relapse, and the decreased, slowed ability to respond to naturally rewarding stimuli. The Diagnostic and Statistical Manual of Mental Disorders, Fourth Edition (DSM-IV) has categorized three stages of addiction: preoccupation/anticipation, binge/intoxication, and withdrawal/negative affect. These stages are characterized, respectively, by constant cravings and preoccupation with obtaining the substance; using more of the substance than necessary to experience the intoxicating effects; and experiencing tolerance, withdrawal symptoms, and decreased motivation for normal life activities. By definition, drug addiction differs from drug dependence and drug tolerance.

Non-biological reasons

Some individuals are at a higher risk of addiction because they lack self-control, have no moral opposition to drugs, have low self-esteem, or are depressed. Research has also shown that individuals who live in isolation or in poverty are more likely to become addicted to drugs. People who associate with drug users are more likely to become users themselves. Drugs that produce a short-lived but intense state of intoxication (cocaine, for instance) are more likely to be addictive, as are those that have especially painful withdrawal symptoms. Most of the people who will experiment with drugs do so during adolescence. Although many have suggested that drugs like alcohol, tobacco, and marijuana lead to use of harder drugs, most research on this subject has been inconclusive.

Variability of addiction

The reasons for drug addiction are a combination of the factors of heredity, environment, the use of psychoactive drugs and the personality of the individual. Because individual personalities, heredity, physiology and lifestyles vary, each person's resistance or susceptibility to drug use also varies. The drug user with a higher biological predisposition for addiction likes the (initial) drug high more than do users who lack this heightened risk. The more important the use of drugs is to anyone, the more rewarding the drug experience, and the greater the risk of addiction. In contrast, many people who experiment with drugs and then discontinue use without ever progressing to having a love affair with it say that the drugs did little or nothing for them. Although it is not possible at this time to test for a genetic trait associated with addiction, it is possible to determine just how much the use of the addictive substance means to the person using it by asking the person. Diversity of risk does not mean that some people are vulnerable to addiction and others are not, but it does mean that some people are relatively more vulnerable than others. A person who starts with a low inherited susceptibility and low environmental stress might need intense use of drugs to push him into addiction. The greater the environmental stress, the fewer drugs are needed to develop addiction. Everyone, however, is susceptible to addiction if exposed often enough.

Variables affecting drug use

The particular effects experienced by a drug user depend on a few different variables: dosage, individual characteristics, and setting. For most drugs, an increase in dosage will intensify the effects of the drug. There may also be a change in the effect experienced from a drug at low dosage than from that same drug at a higher dosage. Every person will respond differently to a drug as well, depending on their psychological and physical state. The enzymes in the bloodstream play a major role in reducing drug levels in the blood, so an individual's drug experience will largely depend on the quality and quantity of his or her enzymes. Many people report a change in the effects of a drug related to their setting; a stressful situation, for instance, may cause the effects of some drugs to be more intense.

Addictive personality

The addictive personality consists of 2 different elements: the Self, which represents the "normal" human side of the addicted person, and the Addict, which represents the human side that is consumed and transformed by the addiction. This personality does not exist prior to the illness of addiction, nor does it represent a predisposition to addiction. Rather, it emerges from the addictive process, in which the Addict becomes the dominant personality. The Addict side within does not care about family and friends. The Addict side does not care about the Self either. What it cares about is acting out and achieving the trance. There is an almost constant conflict between the Self and the Addict when facing the choice of acting out (the search for/consumption of drugs) or not. This great internal tension can go on for hours, days or weeks at a time, and is a large part of the suffering caused by addiction. But in the end of this struggle, the Addict invariably wins. The Self and Addict continue to fight for control: The Self regularly fights and argues with the Addict, but loses. The Self makes promises to control the Addict, uses will power to control the Addict, but loses. We see how the gradual loss of the Self occurs in addiction, and how the Addict slowly gains more and more control. The Self witnesses the addictive ritual and is often sickened by what it is forced to participate in, but it is held captive by the power of the disease of addiction. To fight and struggle against something that has more power than one self drains one's energy. For each defeat there is some loss of self-esteem.

Way of thinking

The Addict develops its own way of thinking; through the development of addictive logic, the Addict side of the individual justifies his drug taking behaviors. Every time the addict chooses to act out in an addictive way, he is saying to himself one or more of the following: "I don't need people." "I don't have to face anything I don't want to." "I'm afraid to face life and my problems." "Drugs are more important than people." "I can do anything I want, no matter whom it hurts." "I want what I want and I want it now." "Even though I had seen what it could do, I thought I would be fine–they were junkies and somehow I was different." "I just use drugs occasionally." "I can stop when I want." This type of thinking continually supports and reinforces an addictive belief system in the addict. It's through the development of addictive logic that the addicted person finds a way to cope with his drug use. Addicts must make sense of this to themselves, and they do so by denying the fear and emotional pain caused by their inappropriate behaviors. After intense episodes of acting out, the addict needs to make sense out of what happened and turns to his delusion system and addictive logic for an answer. This is where the addict turns to denial, repression, lies, rationalizations, and other defenses to help cope with what is happening. Because of the delusion system, it is nearly impossible for addicts to see the true reasons for their addictive behaviors. They believe that they are misunderstood by others, yet in reality they are unable to see their own assault upon themselves.

Addictive logic

Addictive logic is not based on truth, but on the delusion of the addictive relationship. Addictive logic denies the presence of an addictive relationship. Addictive logic says it is alright to hurt one's Self because the Self is not important – it's the mood change or trance that counts. Addictive logic says it is all right to hurt others because relationships with people are not important. What is important is a relationship with the drug. Once addicted, people feel that drug use has become a matter of survival.

Addict behavior

The addict develops his own way of behaving. As addiction develops, it becomes a way of life. In addicts, drugs fill a central role in life: addicts have learned to use drugs to fulfill almost all needs, especially emotional needs. There are many ways a person's behavior adapts to the addictive process, bringing about an addictive lifestyle. The addict may display inappropriate and irresponsible behaviors in several ways: Examples: "Often, I love my mother, but I rob her, I want to please and serve my employer, but I abuse his confidence, I love my drug using friends, but I betray them." "I found I was taking money meant to buy presents for my children." "I knew I hit a low point when I used toilet water to shoot up." The addict may lie to others, even when it is easier to tell the truth. The addict may blame others, knowing others are not to blame. The addict may ritualize his/her behaviors.

Rituals

Rituals are a language of behaviors. In addiction, rituals become value statements about the beliefs of the addict. Each time a person acts out, his/her addictive belief system is strengthened. Addictive rituals push a person deeper into the addictive process. Addicts may become fanatics about their rituals. Rituals are based on consistency: first you do this, and then you do that. Addicts ritualize their behavior for the comfort found in predictability. Each part of the rite is important to the addict and is designed to heighten the mood change. When addicts face crisis and stress, they run to the comfort they find in their rituals. The pain- free state lasts as long as the individual remains in the mood change created by the addictive ritual. But the trance always fades away and sensations always disappear, leaving the addict with the original pain plus the loss of the pleasurable sensations. Addicts no longer put faith in people, but in their addictive rite. Addictive rituals most often take place alone or within a group whose members have no real caring connection to each other.

Addictive process

The addictive process is a cycle downwards, which may lead to destruction. Addiction occurs gradually and must be viewed as a progressive and continually changing process. Over time, addicts give up more and more of their lives that do not involve the addiction itself. Addiction becomes worse over time, slowly or rapidly, until there are painful and inescapable consequences of drug use. This phase is called "hitting bottom." Over time, bottoms become more severe, or lower, as the disease worsens. Commonly, addicts hit a painful bottom, decide to stop drug use and then slip back into denial and use once more, only to encounter new, lower bottoms. It is said that "when you do drugs, you burn up all your resources. Finally there is nowhere to go, no money left and no one to call." Experience of emotional pain and/or discomfort leads to acting out (search for/use of drugs), which gives momentary and temporary pleasure, resulting in the experience of more emotional pain, when the effects of the drug fade away. Feeling power when using drugs leads to a momentary and temporary feeling of being in control and being right, resulting in feeling out of control when the effects of the drug fade, which as a consequence demands more power (by using drugs) to alleviate the negative feelings of being out of control. These addictive cycles are endless unless the addict seeks help. Once the addict surrenders to the need for help, the process of recovery and the renewal of the Self may begin.

The following are determining factors in the possible evolution of drug use to addiction:

- Positive relationships
- Parental monitoring and support
- High academic performance
- Anti-drug policies in schools and communities
- Strong neighborhood attachment
- Self-Control
- Isolation
- Early drug use
- High Potency of the drug
- Frequent drug use
- High amount of drug use
- Smoking or injecting a drug
- Mental illness
- Exposure to physical or sexual abuse
- Early aggressive behavior

Gateway drug theory

The gateway drug theory is the belief that use of a lower classed drug can lead to the subsequent use of "harder", more dangerous drugs. The term is also used to describe introductory experiences to addictive substances. Some believe tobacco, alcohol, and marijuana are gateway drugs. Some research suggests that serious drug abusers adopt an atypical drug use sequence with use of other drugs initiated before marijuana or alcohol. There are many pharmacological similarities between various drugs of abuse. Individual social histories show that "hard" drug users do progress from one drug to another, but the reasons are not clear enough to generalize a gateway.

Intoxication, withdrawal, polyabuse, and comorbidity

In clinical terms, intoxication is the behavioral, psychological, and physiological changes that occur in a drug user. In the beginning stages of drug addiction, the goal is usually intoxication. Later in the addiction process, however, the goal of use tends to be avoiding withdrawal symptoms. Withdrawal is any physiological distress that occurs because a drug is not taken. Many drug abusers take several different drugs, though they may prefer only one; this condition is known as polyabuse. Studies have also shown that there is a significant overlap between people with chemical dependencies and people with psychological disorders. This overlap is known as comorbidity, and in part accounts for the profound problems that many drug abusers face in trying to escape their addictions.

Psychological and physical dependence

A psychological dependence on drugs may begin as a craving for the pleasurable feelings or relief from anxiety that the drug provides. However, this craving can soon turn into a dependency on the drug in order to perform normal mental operations. A physical dependency, on the other hand, is said to occur when the individual requires increasing amounts of the drug to get the desired effect. Many drugs, like marijuana or hallucinogens, do not cause withdrawal symptoms; others, like heroin or cocaine, may be extremely painful to stop using. Individuals with a severe chemical dependency will eventually use a drug like this simply to avoid experiencing the effects of withdrawal. Typically, an individual with a severe dependency will try to stop many times without success.

Addiction-causing drugs

Drugs known to cause addiction include illegal drugs as well as prescription or over-the-counter drugs.

- Stimulants
    - o Amphetamine and Methamphetamine
    - o Caffeine
    - o Cocaine
    - o Nicotine
- Sedatives and Hypnotics
    - o Alcohol
    - o Barbiturates
    - o Benzodiazepines, particularly alprazolam, clonazepam, temazepam, and nimetazepam
    - o Methaqualone and the related quinazolinone sedative-hypnotics
    - o GHB and analogues (specifically GBL)
    - o Opiate and Opioid analgesics
    - o Morphine and Codeine, the two naturally-occurring opiate analgesics
    - o Semi-synthetic opiates, such as Heroin (Diacetylmorphine), Oxycodone, and Hydromorphone
    - o Fully synthetic opioids, such as Fentanyl and its analogs, Meperidine/Pethidine, and Methadone
- Anabolic steroids

The most common drug addictions are to legal substances such as:
- Alcohol

- Nicotine in the form of tobacco, particularly cigarettes

Hazards of illicit drug use

Among the hazards of illicit drug use is the ever-increasing risk of infection, disease, and overdose. While pharmaceutical products have a known concentration and purity, clandestinely produced street drugs have unknown compositions. Medical complications common among narcotic abusers arise primarily from adulterants found in street drugs and in the non-sterile practices of injecting. Skin, lung, and brain abscesses, endocarditis, hepatitis, and AIDS are commonly found among narcotic abusers. As the purity of a street drug is indeterminable, the effects of illicit narcotic use are unpredictable and can be fatal. Physical signs of narcotic overdose include constricted (pinpoint) pupils, cold clammy skin, confusion, convulsions, severe drowsiness, and respiratory depression (slow or troubled breathing). With repeated use of narcotics, tolerance and dependence develop. The development of tolerance is characterized by a shortened duration and a decreased intensity of analgesia, euphoria, and sedation, which creates the need to consume progressively larger doses to attain the desired effect. This tolerance leads to physical dependence, which necessitates the continued presence of a drug in order to prevent a withdrawal or abstinence syndrome. The intensity and character of the physical symptoms experienced during withdrawal are directly related to the particular drug of abuse, the total daily dose, the interval between doses, the duration of use, and the health and personality of the user. Although unpleasant, withdrawal from narcotics is rarely life threatening.

Addictive potency of drugs

The addictive potency of drugs varies from substance to substance, and from individual to individual. Drugs such as codeine or alcohol, for instance, typically require many more exposures to addict their users than drugs such as heroin or cocaine. Likewise, a person who is psychologically or genetically predisposed to addiction is much more likely to suffer from it. Although dependency on hallucinogens like LSD ("acid") and psilocybin (key hallucinogen in "magic mushrooms") is listed as Substance-Related Disorder in the DSM-IV, most psychologists do not classify them as addictive drugs.

Effects of chronic drug use

The effects of habitual drug use can be either chronic (resulting from long-term use) or acute (resulting from a single dose). Acute effects are usually determined by the particular drug; first-time users of stimulants, for instance, may be overcome with a powerful sense of anger. The effects of chronic drug use are more predictable. Over a long period of time, consistent drug users may feel tired, lose weight, have a nagging cough, and develop overall body aches. Drug abusers often suffer from blackouts and may undergo psychological turmoil and bouts of paranoia. Typically, the stress involved with supporting and maintaining a habit increases over time, and this stress adds to the damage done by the drug itself.

Allostasis

The concept of allostasis is the process of achieving stability through changes in behavior as well as physiological features. Allostasis appears to adjust as a person progresses into drug addiction and enters a new allostatic state, defined as divergence from normal levels of change which persist in a chronic state. Addiction to drugs can cause damage to your brain and body as you enter the pathological state; the cost stemming from damage is known as allostatic load. The deregulation of allostasis gradually occurs as the reward from the drug decreases and the ability to overcome the depressed state following drug use begins to decrease as well. The resulting allostatic load creates a constant state of depression relative to normal allostatic changes. What pushes this decrease is the propensity of drug users to take the drug before the brain and body have returned to original allostatic levels, producing a constant state of stress. Therefore, environmental stressors may induce stronger drug seeking behaviors than in the presence of no environmental stressors.

Learning and behavior

Understanding how learning and behavior work in the reward circuit can help understand the action of addictive drugs. Drug addiction is characterized by strong, drug seeking behaviors in which the addict persistently craves and seeks out drugs, despite the knowledge of harmful consequences. Addictive drugs produce a reward, which is the euphoric feeling resulting from sustained DA concentrations in the synaptic cleft of neurons in the brain. Operant conditioning is exhibited in drug addicts as well as laboratory mice, rats, and primates; they are able to associate an action or behavior, in this case seeking out the drug, with a reward, which is the effect of the drug. Evidence shows that this behavior is most likely a result of the synaptic changes which have occurred due to repeated drug exposure. The drug seeking behavior is induced by glutamatergic projections from the prefrontal cortex to the NAc. This idea is supported with data from experiments showing the drug seeking behavior can be prevented following the inhibition of AMPA glutamate receptors and glutamate release in the NAc.

Stress

<u>Stress, stressors, eustress and distress</u>
Stress can be a rather vague word, and so it needs to be defined in the context of health education. In this setting, stress refers to the response that the body makes to any demand placed upon it. These demands may be physical, mental, or emotional. The things that are creating these demands are called stressors. Stressors can be academic examinations, health problems, heavy physical loads, or even happy occasions. Eustress is the term used by health professionals to describe

positive stress; that is, stress that encourages the individual to adapt, grow, or develop. The opposite of eustress is distress, the negative forms of stress. Distress is stress that is harmful to the individual, and in some way prevents him or her from living to potential.

Signs of a stress problem

Many individuals become so used to the high amount of stress in their lives that they become used to it and don't try and remedy the situation. There are a few warning signs that stress may be a problem. For instance, individuals experiencing chronic fatigue, headaches, diarrhea, indigestion, or sleep problems may be over-stressed. Self-medication, including the use of non-prescription drugs, can be a sign that stress has reached a problematic level. Individuals under stress frequently have a hard time concentrating, and may feel irritable or apathetic. They also tend to exaggerate the importance of their work to others, and can become more prone to accidents. Stressed individuals often exhibit extreme behavior, for instance in eating, drinking, or working.

Mood management

Moods are emotional states lasting for a few hours or days. Though every individual will have bad moods from time to time, some are better at managing their moods than others. Researchers have demonstrated that the most effective ways to solve a problem, and hence emerge from a bad mood, are to take immediate action, think about other successes, resolve to try harder, or reward oneself. Individuals who try to distract themselves, perhaps through socializing, will find that this only partly improves their mood. The worst things to do when you are in a bad mood are to vent at another person, isolate yourself, or give up. Using alcohol or drugs to escape a bad mood is also an ineffective way to feel better.

Alcohol and drug use disorders

Alcohol and drug use disorders—which include misuse, dependence, or addiction to alcohol and/or legal or illegal drugs—remain a major public health problem in the United States. The social cost of alcohol and drug use in the United States is staggering, estimated at more than $294 billion in 1997. More than 9 percent of the total population age 12 or older met the criteria for substance dependence or abuse in 2002. An estimated 19.5 million Americans (8.3 percent of the population age 12 or older) were current users of illicit drugs in 2002, meaning they had used an illicit drug at least once during the month prior to being interviewed. About 54 million Americans in 2002 (nearly 23 percent of the population age 12 or older) said they had participated in binge drinking (5 or more drinks on the same occasion) at least once in the last 30 days. Nearly 16 million said they were heavy drinkers (had 5 or more drinks on the same occasion on at least 5 days during the past month). Alcohol and drug use disorders can affect anyone. But those who are particularly vulnerable include people with a co-occurring mental disorder or those who have certain risk factors, including poverty or a family history of alcohol or drug use disorders. Alcohol and drug use disorders affect not just the people who are in need of treatment, but also their family members. Clearly, the effects of helping one person achieve recovery from an alcohol or drug use disorder can improve a multitude of lives.

Public health practitioners have attempted to look at drug abuse from a broader perspective than the individual, emphasizing the role of society, culture and availability. Rather than accepting the loaded terms alcohol or drug "abuse," many public health professionals have adopted phrases such as "alcohol and drug problems" or "harmful/problematic use" of drugs.

Youth

More than 36 percent of American 17-year-olds reported current alcohol use in 2002, and more than 11 percent of youths ages 12 to 17 reported current illicit drug use. Some children are using drugs at age 12 or 13, and others may begin earlier. But families can help prevent alcohol and drug use disorders by creating strong bonds with their children, setting clear limits, and being actively involved with their children's lives. As many as one in four children—19 million children or 28.6 percent of children under the age of 18—lives in a home where problems with alcohol are a fact of daily life. Use of marijuana, Ecstasy, LSD, cigarettes, and alcohol decreased significantly from 2001 to 2002 among 8th, 10th, and 12th grade students in U.S. schools.

Senior adults

Inadvertent misuse of prescription drugs is common among the elderly, who use prescription drugs three times more often than the general population does, and who may have difficulty complying with directions for taking a medication. Misuse of prescription drugs can lead to complications, including memory loss. Only about 14 percent of treatment facilities have addiction treatment programs designed specifically for older adults.

Men vs. women and people of color

Men are twice as likely as women to be considered to have an alcohol or drug use disorder, except among youths ages 12 to 17, when the prevalence of alcohol or drug use disorders is relatively the same for both genders.

The rates of current illicit drug use in 2002 were highest among American Indians/Alaska Natives (10.1 percent) and people of mixed race (made up of two or more races) (11.4 percent). Rates of illicit drug use were 9.7 percent for blacks, 8.5 percent for whites, and 7.2 percent for Hispanics. Asians had the lowest rate at 3.5 percent. The impact of alcohol and drug use disorders is much greater than these numbers indicate. Alcohol and drug use disorders affect not just the people suffering from them, but also family members (particularly the children of those affected), friends, co-workers, and others who interact with them.

<u>Worldwide</u>

Drug abuse has a wide range of definitions related to taking a psychoactive drug or performance enhancing drug for a non-therapeutic or non-medical effect. Some of the most commonly abused drugs include alcohol, amphetamines, barbiturates, benzodiazepines, cocaine, methaqualone, and opium alkaloids. Use of these drugs may lead to criminal penalty in addition to possible physical, social, and psychological harm, both strongly depending on local jurisdiction. Other definitions of drug abuse fall into four main categories: public health definitions, mass communication and vernacular usage, medical definitions, and political and criminal justice definitions. An estimated 4.7% of the global population aged 15 to 64, or 185 million people, consume illicit drugs annually.

Underground talk of drugs

Drugs are illegal in most places in the world today. For this reason talk of it has had to go underground. A very effective way of going underground is the development of a secret code language known and understood only by those who live in that world. In this way people can talk about illicit drug taking right in front of partners and parents without fear of them catching on. Like any language that boasts a number of users drug related street terms are now more numerous than can begin to be recorded or described. There is also nothing static about this street slang. It changes faster than fashion and prides itself on staying ahead of those who would crack the code.

Teenage drug use

The most popular functions for drug use are using to: relax (96.7%), become intoxicated (96.4%), keep awake at night while socializing (95.9%), enhance an activity (88.5%) and alleviate depressed mood (86.8%). Substance use functions were found to differ by age and gender. Targeting substances that are perceived to fulfill similar functions and addressing issues concerning the substitution of one substance for another may also strengthen education and prevention efforts. Family dysfunction and peer pressure usually prompt teen boys to begin experimenting with drugs, but for girls genetic factors play a much greater role, according to a published study. "In girls, there was a significant genetic influence on all substance abuse in adolescence," Judy Silberg, the lead author of the study, told the Chicago Sun-Times. "There was no significant effect of the genes on drug use in boys." Silberg says the results of her study demonstrate that the same tactics should not be used to prevent drug abuse in boys and girls.

The Center for Disease Control maintains that adolescent drug abuse is an ongoing problem that needs to be addressed. Besides the health risks associated with the drugs themselves, the CDC asserts that persistent drug use contributes to failure in school, fights, antisocial behavior, and unintentional injuries. Prolonged drug use can also be responsible for depression and anxiety. The CDC also maintains that drug use contributes to the HIV epidemic, insofar as those who share needles are liable to contract the virus, and drug users in general tend to engage in risky sexual behaviors. The statistics kept by the CDC state that marijuana use among teenagers decreased from 26% to 22% between 1997 and 2003.

Recreational and responsible drug use

Recreational drug use is the use of psychoactive drugs for recreational purposes rather than for work, medical, or spiritual purposes, although the distinction is not always clear. At least one psychopharmacologist who has studied this field refers to it as the 'Fourth Drive,' arguing that the human instinct to seek mind-altering substances has so much force and persistence that it functions like the human drives for hunger, thirst, and shelter.

The concept of responsible drug use is that a person can use recreational drugs with reduced or eliminated risk of negatively affecting other parts of one's life or other people's lives. Advocates of this philosophy point to the many well-known artists and intellectuals who have used drugs, experimentally or otherwise, with few detrimental effects on their lives. Critics argue that the drugs are escapist, and dangerous, unpredictable, and sometimes addictive; thus predicating the idea of a responsible use of drugs as an idea, ultimately disputable upon debate.

Costs of drug addiction

The costs of drug addiction on the users themselves, their families, and society as a whole are incredibly high. All illegal drug abuse lowers inhibition and promotes antisocial behavior. Even when drug abusers do not inject drugs, they are at increased risk of HIV infection because of other high-risk behaviors, especially promiscuous sexual activities. Drugs, by changing the personality and impulse control, can therefore induce criminal acts. Some drug abusers and addicts resort to violence either to fund their habits or as a result of the psycho-pharmacological impact of some illicit drugs. Drug addiction is most often accompanied by multiple drug use, with related consequences of the different drugs involved. Drug addiction often co-occurs with many psychiatric disorders.

Abuse liability

Abuse liability is the propensity of a particular psychoactive substance to be susceptible to abuse, defined in terms of the relative probability that use of the substance will result in social, psychological, or physical problems for an individual or for society. A wide variety of prescription drugs, proprietary (OTC) drugs, and herbal and folk remedies may be involved. The particularly important groups are:

- Psychotropic drugs that do not produce dependence, such as antidepressants and neuroleptics.
- Laxatives (misuse of which is termed the "laxative habit").
- Analgesics that may be purchased without medical prescription, such as aspirin and Tylenol (acetaminophen).
- Steroids and other hormones.
- Vitamins.
- Antacids.

These substances do not typically have pleasurable psychic effects, yet attempts to discourage or forbid their use are met with resistance. Despite the patient's strong motivation to take the substance, neither the dependence syndrome nor the withdrawal syndrome develops. These substances do not have dependence potential in the sense of intrinsic pharmacological effects, but are capable of inducing psychological dependence.

Codependence

A codependent individual is one who allows someone with an addiction to use them to achieve satisfaction. Codependency causes a person to ignore his or her own needs in order to serve someone else's. They will change their identity, undergo unpleasant experiences, and even give up their friends and family in order to serve the other. People with low self-esteem and their own set of addictions are more likely to become codependent. In order to escape from a codependent relationship, an individual must realize the worth of his or her own life as well as his or her inability to change the other person. Codependent behavior has at its heart a simple desire for love, though this desire is poorly expressed.

Enabling

Enabling is any behavior performed by a codependent individual that allows the partner to satisfy an addiction. Enabling comes in a few different forms. Shielding is when a codependent person keeps their partner safe from the negative consequences of their action, by making excuses or covering for them. Controlling is when one person tries to bribe the other with sexual favors in exchange for reducing an addictive behavior. Sometimes, a codependent may enable by assuming an unfair share of household responsibilities. Other times, a codependent may rationalize the addictive behavior of the other, and therefore not see it clearly. Some enablers become intimately involved in the self-destructive behavior of the other, placing bets or procuring drugs for them. Finally, a codependent may facilitate the safe use of an addictive substance, by allowing the user to do it at home.

General laws concerning controlled substances and tobacco

For the most part, the law of the United States takes a stern view of the growth, use, and distribution of controlled substances, such as marijuana, cocaine, and heroin. These drugs are illegal in any quantity, and individuals carrying a certain minimum amount can be charged with possession with intent to sell, which carries a much stiffer penalty. Individuals will also receive a much stiffer penalty if they are discovered carrying drugs across state lines. The minimum age for purchasing tobacco products is 18 years of age in most states. Retail carriers can be fined substantially for selling to underage individuals. Moreover, more places are becoming off-limits to smoking every year; recently, the city of New York banned smoking in all of its bars and restaurants.

Drinking and driving

The most common crime in the United States is drinking and driving. In order to combat this menace to public safety, many communities offer free rides to people who have had too much to drink. Police frequently set up checkpoints along major roads, so that they can check drivers for the signs of intoxication. There has also been a move to increase the legal consequences of a drunk-driving ticket, and many states revoke a license for the first offence. Currently, all states have conformed to the federal standard of having a BAC level of 0.08% or higher as the legal definition of intoxicated or drunk driving. Most drunk drivers are single men between the ages of 25 and 45.

Sedatives and crime

The sedatives GHB, Flunitrazepam (Rohypnol®), and to a lesser extent, temazepam (Restoril®), and midazolam (Versed®) are known for their use as date rape drugs (also called a Mickey), administered to unsuspecting patrons in bars or guests at parties to reduce the intended victims' defenses. These drugs are also used for robbing people; indeed statistical overviews suggest that the use of sedative-spiked drinks for robbing people is actually much more common than their use for rape. These drugs are also known as "mug drugs". Cases of criminals taking rohypnol themselves before they commit crimes have also been reported, as the loss of inhibitions from the drug may increase their confidence to commit the offence, and the amnesia produced by the drug makes it difficult for police to interrogate them if they are caught.

Arguments for drug prohibition

Many of the arguments for drug prohibition are based on perceptions of drugs as dangerous to people, which creates the basis for a moral opposition to drug use.

Some of these perceptions are based on common knowledge or scientific evidence, indicating how certain drugs are detrimental to individuals and communities, while other perceptions are based on popular myths. Those who are against prohibition argue that even when drugs are dangerous to people, it is much easier to control their use and minimize harm if drugs are legal. The decriminalization of drugs would then be perceived as a more ethical way to deal with the problem.

Drug control legislation

Depending on the jurisdiction, addictive drugs may be legal only as part of a government sponsored study, illegal to use for any purpose, illegal to sell, or even illegal to merely possess. Most countries have legislation which brings various drugs and drug-like substances under the control of licensing systems. Typically this legislation covers any or all of the opiates, amphetamines, cannabinoids, cocaine, barbiturates, hallucinogenics and a variety of more modern synthetic drugs, and unlicensed production, supply or possession is a criminal offence. Usually, however, drug classification under such legislation is not related simply to addictiveness. The substances covered often have very different addictive properties. Some are highly prone to cause physical dependency, while others rarely cause any form of compulsive need whatsoever. Also, under legislation specifically about drugs, alcohol is not usually included.

<u>Negative effects of criminalizing drugs</u>
Although the legislation may be justifiable on moral or public health grounds, it can make addiction or dependency a much more serious issue for the individual: reliable supplies of a drug become difficult to secure, and the individual becomes vulnerable to both criminal abuse and legal punishment. It is unclear whether laws against drugs do anything to stem usage and dependency. In jurisdictions where addictive drugs are illegal, they are generally supplied by drug dealers, who are often involved with organized crime. Even though the cost of producing most illegal

addictive substances is very low, their illegality combined with the addict's need permits the seller to command a premium price, often hundreds of times the production cost. As a result, the addict sometimes turns to crime to support their habit.

CSA updates

The Controlled Substances Act (CSA) is the principal federal law directed at combating the illicit manufacture and distribution of controlled drugs in the United States. Since its passage in 1970, the CSA has been amended. The most recent change in the scope of the CSA is the implementation of amendments and regulations regarding chemicals and equipment used in the illicit production of controlled substances. The clandestine production of drugs is dependent on the availability of chemicals necessary to accomplish the illicit activity. Most of the drugs in the illicit traffic, with the exception of marijuana, require chemicals to be produced. The controls placed on chemicals are substantially less than those imposed on controlled drugs because most of the chemicals have legitimate industrial applications. For this reason, the term "regulated" more appropriately describes chemicals covered under the CSA as compared to the term "controlled" that is used for drugs. Several items that are regulated as chemicals under the CSA are also non-controlled ingredients in drug products lawfully marketed under the Federal Food, Drug and Cosmetic Act and are, therefore, widely available to the general public. Examples of these products include over-the-counter (OTC) medications containing ephedrine, pseudoephedrine, and/or phenylpropanolamine.

Drugs and child abuse/neglect

Drug use and drug addiction leads to child abuse and neglect. Drugs are involved in 7 out of 10 cases of child abuse and neglect. For example, children in cannabis grow houses are at risk not only from the chemicals and often dangerous electrical hookups that are used to grow dope but also from the threat of armed home invasion by thieves looking to rip off the marijuana or any available cash on hand.

Parenting a child with drug abuse issues

Parents must make clear that drug use will not be tolerated. Children need to understand that parents are concerned because they love them. Parents need to set a positive example and get involved in their children's lives and know what they're doing. Drug using teens are unlikely to admit drug use because they often are in denial that they have a problem. Why would you worry or get treated when you're doing something you enjoy doing? Drug testing cuts through the denial of drug using children.

Brain damage in teens

Early drug use is linked to later depression in teen girls, but in boys the study found no evidence that drug use leads to depression, or that depression leads to drug use. Young drug abusers are up to three times more likely to suffer brain damage than those who do not use drugs. Scientists at the University of Edinburgh studied the brains of 34 deceased intravenous drug abusers of heroin and methadone and compared them to the brains of 16 young people who were not drug users. Their examination revealed brain damage in the drug abusers normally seen in much older people. The damaged nerve cells were in the areas of the brain involved in learning, memory and emotional well being, and were similar to damage found in the early stages of Alzheimer's disease. The study showed evidence of an increased risk of brain damage associated with heroin and methadone use, which may be highest in the young, when individuals are most likely to acquire the habit.

It was found that the brains of these young drug abusers showed significantly higher levels of two key proteins associated with brain damage. In a previous study it was found that drug abuse causes low grade inflammation in the brain. Taken together, the two studies suggest that intravenous opiate abuse may be linked to premature aging of the brain.

The drug abusers who were examined in the study sadly died at a young age, but there are many others who do not realize the long-term effects that these drugs may be causing.

Environmental damage

Drug use and drug addiction induce environmental damage. Illegal drug use is detrimental for our precious nature on earth. In South-America, many acres of rainforest are destroyed due to cocaine cultivation. In Morocco, the monoculture of cannabis is dangerous for the ecosystem, especially because the farmers are making an extensive use of noxious fertilizers and pesticides. Forested areas, which are among the specificities of the Rif area, are destroyed to accommodate new cannabis fields, thus accelerating soil erosion. Methamphetamine and ecstasy labs are throwing tons of chemical waste in the environment. Cannabis cultivation requires a lot of water. Water is derived to the cannabis cultivation, resulting in less water supply for food crops and soil erosion, leading to the progression of the desert, Afghanistan being one example. Food shortages in Africa are becoming more serious because of a shift from growing food crops to cultivating cannabis. A higher global demand of drugs by drug users and drug addicts results in an incremental production of drugs which leads to the accelerated destruction of the environment.

Important terms

Administration, method of route, or mode of administration: the way in which a substance is introduced into the body, such as oral ingestion, intravenous (IV), subcutaneous, or intramuscular injection, inhalation, smoking, or absorption through skin or mucosal surfaces, such as the gums, rectum, or genitalia.

Adverse drug reaction: In the general medical and pharmacological fields, denotes a toxic physical or (less commonly) psychological reaction to a therapeutic agent. The reaction may be predictable, allergic, or idiosyncratic (unpredictable). In the context of substance use, the term includes unpleasant psychological or physical reactions to drug taking.

Affective disorder, residual, alcohol-, or drug-related: Alcohol- or drug-induced changes in affect that persist beyond the period during which a direct effect of the alcohol or drug might reasonably be assumed to be operating.

Amethyst Agent: a substance taken with the objective of reversing or mitigating the intoxicating effects of alcohol. Such compounds may act by inhibiting the effects of alcohol on the central nervous system or by accelerating the metabolism of alcohol by the liver. Effective drugs of this class are not currently available for therapeutic purposes.

Common street language

Serial speedballing: Sequencing cocaine, cough syrup and heroin over a 1 to 2 day period.

A-boot: Under the influence of drugs

Agonies: Withdrawal symptoms

Chalked up: Under the influence of cocaine

Heaven and Hell: PCP

Pharming: Consuming mixture of prescription substances

Tardust: Cocaine

Tweak mission: On a mission to find crack

Wake ups: Amphetamines

Sacrament: LSD

Highbeams: Wide eyes associated with taking crack

Paperbag: Container for drugs

Tex-Mex: Marijuana

Sam: Federal narcotics agent

Carpet patrol: Crack smokers searching the floor for crack

Half a football field: 50 rocks of crack

Amphead: LSD user

Author: Doctor who writes illegal prescriptions

Are you anywhere: Do you use marijuana

Closet baser: User of cocaine that prefers anonymity

Honeymoon: Early stages of drug use before addiction

Miss: To inject a drug

Hype stick: Hypodermic needle

Piggybacking: Simultaneous injecting of two different drugs

Toke: To inhale cocaine or smoke marijuana

Classification of Drugs

Controlled Substance Act

In 1969, President Nixon announced that the Attorney General was preparing a comprehensive new measure to more effectively meet the narcotic and dangerous drug problems at the Federal level by combining all existing federal laws into a single new statute. According to David T. Courtwright, "the 1970 Controlled Substances Act was part of an omnibus reform package designed to rationalize, and in some respects to liberalize, American drug policy." It eliminated mandatory minimum sentences and provided support for drug treatment and research. King notes that the rehabilitation clauses were added as a compromise to Senator Hughes, who favored a moderate approach. While the bill was being drafted, the Uniform Controlled Substances Act, to be passed by state legislatures, was also being drafted by the Department of Justice; its wording closely mirrored the Controlled Substances Act.

The Controlled Substances Act (CSA) was enacted into law by the Congress of the United States as Title II of the Comprehensive Drug Abuse Prevention and Control Act of 1970. The CSA is the legal basis by which the manufacture, importation, possession, and distribution of certain drugs are regulated by the federal government of the United States. The Act also served as the national implementing legislation for the Single Convention on Narcotic Drugs. The legislation created five Schedules (classifications), with varying qualifications for a drug to be included in each. Two federal departments, the Department of Justice and the Department of Health and Human Services (which includes the Food and Drug Administration) determine which drugs are added or removed from the various schedules, though the statute passed by Congress created the initial listing. Classification decisions are required to be made on the criteria of potential for abuse, accepted medical use in the United States, and potential for dependence. The Department of Justice is also the executive agency in charge of federal law enforcement. State governments also regulate certain drugs not controlled at the federal level.

Congressional findings state that a major purpose of the CSA is to "enable the United States to meet all of its obligations" under international treaties—specifically, the 1961 Single Convention on Narcotic Drugs and the 1971 Convention on Psychotropic Substances. Both the CSA and these treaties set out a system for classifying controlled substances in several Schedules in accordance with the binding scientific and medical findings of a public health authority; In the US, the Secretary of Health and Human Services (HHS), and under the two aforementioned conventions, the World Health Organization. A provision for automatic compliance with treaty obligations is found at 21 U.S.C. § 811(d), which also establishes mechanisms for amending international drug control regulations to correspond with HHS findings on scientific and medical issues. If control of a substance is mandated by the Single Convention, the Attorney General is required to "issue an order controlling such drug under the schedule he deems most appropriate to carry out such obligations," without regard to the normal scheduling procedure or the findings of the HHS Secretary. However, the Secretary has great influence over any drug scheduling proposal under the Single Convention, because 21 U.S.C. § 811(d)(2)(B) gives the Secretary the power to "evaluate the proposal and furnish a recommendation to the Secretary of State which shall be binding on the representative of the United States in discussions and negotiations relating to the proposal."

Since its enactment in 1970, the Act has been amended several times:
- The Psychotropic Substances Act of 1978 added provisions implementing the Convention on Psychotropic Substances.
- The Controlled Substances Penalties Amendments Act of 1984.

- The Chemical Diversion and Trafficking Act of 1988 added provisions implementing the United Nations Convention Against Illicit Traffic in Narcotic Drugs and Psychotropic Substances.
- The Domestic Chemical Diversion and Control Act of 1993.
- The Federal Analog Act.

Scientific evaluations

The medical and scientific evaluations are binding to the DEA with respect to scientific and medical matters. The recommendation on scheduling is binding only to the extent that if HHS recommends that the substance not be controlled, the DEA may not control the substance. Once the DEA has received the scientific and medical evaluation from HHS, the DEA Administrator will evaluate all available data and make a final decision whether to propose that a drug or other substance be controlled and into which schedule it should be placed. The CSA also creates a closed system of distribution for those authorized to handle controlled substances. The cornerstone of this system is the registration of all those authorized by the DEA to handle controlled substances. All individuals and firms that are registered are required to maintain complete and accurate inventories and records of all transactions involving controlled substances, as well as security for the storage of controlled substances.

Schedule classifications

The findings that the government must make in order to classify a drug in a certain schedule are specified at 21 U.S.C. § 812(b). The specific classification of any given drug is usually a source of controversy, as is the purpose and effectiveness of the entire regulatory scheme. Tobacco, beer, wine, and spirits are explicitly exempt from the Controlled Substances Act. Some have argued that this is an important omission, since alcohol and tobacco are the two most widely abused drugs in the

United States and have no accepted medical uses. Caffeine is also not on the list, although it is a psychoactive drug and it technically meets the requirements for schedule IV or V: it is often abused and it can lead to limited physical dependence. This is largely a result of the substantial political and economic investments in these drugs.

Proceedings to add, delete, or change the schedule of a drug or other substance may be initiated by the Drug Enforcement Administration (DEA), the Department of Health and Human Services (HHS), or by petition from any interested party. When a petition is received by the DEA, the agency begins its own investigation of the drug. The DEA also may begin an investigation of a drug at any time based upon information received from laboratories, state and local law enforcement and regulatory agencies, or other sources of information. Once the DEA has collected the necessary data, the DEA Administrator, by authority of the Attorney General, requests from HHS a scientific and medical evaluation and recommendation as to whether the drug or other substance should be controlled or removed from control. This request is sent to the Assistant Secretary of Health of HHS. Then, HHS solicits information from the Commissioner of the FDA and evaluations and recommendations from the National Institute on Drug Abuse and, on occasion, from the scientific and medical community at large. The Assistant Secretary then compiles the information and transmits back to the DEA a medical and scientific evaluation regarding the drug or other substance, a recommendation as to whether the drug should be controlled, and in which schedule it should be placed.

Schedule I drugs
The requirements to label a drug Schedule I are as follows:
- The drug or other substance has high potential for abuse.
- The drug or other substance has no currently accepted medical use in treatment in the United States.

- There is a lack of accepted safety for use of the drug or other substance under medical supervision.

No prescriptions may be written for Schedule I substances, and such substances are subject to production quotas by the DEA. Under the DEA's interpretation of the CSA, a drug does not necessarily need the same abuse potential as heroin or cocaine to merit placement in Schedule I.

When it comes to a drug that is currently listed in schedule I, if it is undisputed that such drug has no currently accepted medical use in treatment in the United States and a lack of accepted safety for use under medical supervision, and it is further undisputed that the drug has at least some potential for abuse sufficient to warrant control under the CSA, the drug must remain in schedule I. In such circumstances, placement of the drug in schedules II through V would conflict with the CSA since such drug would not meet the criterion of "a currently accepted medical use in treatment in the United States." 21 USC 812(b). Sentences for first-time, non-violent offenders convicted of trafficking in Schedule I drugs can easily turn into de facto life sentences when multiple sales are prosecuted in one proceeding. Sentences for violent offenders are much higher.

Several Schedule I drugs are listed below:
- Methaqualone (Quaalude, Sopor, Mandrax), a sedative that was previously used for similar purposes as barbiturates, until it was rescheduled.
- 2,5-dimethoxy-4-methylamphetamine (STP / DOM), a psychotropic hallucinogen that rose to prominence in 1967 in San Francisco when it appeared in pill form (known as "STP", in doses as high as four times the amounts previously considered "safe") on the black market.
- Tetrahydrogestrinone (THG / "The Clear"), an anabolic progestegenic androgen first created by the BALCO athletic supplement company that was the drug of choice for athletes using steroids due to its "invisibility" in standard steroid screening tests until 2003.

- 2C-B (Nexus / Bees / Venus / Bromo Mescaline), a psychotropic hallucinogen and aphrodisiac.

- AMT (alpha-methyltryptamine), an anti-depressant from the tryptamine family with hallucinogenic properties; first developed in the Soviet Union and marketed under the brand name Indopan;

- Bufotenin (5-OH-DMT), a naturally-occurring tryptamine with hallucinogenic and aphrodisiac properties; named for the Bufo genus of toads whose venom contains the chemical

- Controlled Substance Analogs intended for human consumption (as defined by the Federal Analog Act).

- Lysergic acid diethylamide (LSD / Acid), a psychotropic hallucinogen which has historically been used to treat alcoholism and other addictions, cluster headaches, and has been shown to be useful in treating schizophrenia, Bipolar disorder, childhood autism, and other psychological disorders.

- Peyote, a cactus growing in nature primarily in northeastern Mexico; one of the few plants specifically scheduled, with a narrow exception to its illegal status for religious use by members of the Native American Church.

- Mescaline, the main psychoactive ingredients of the peyote, San Pedro, and Peruvian torch cacti.

- GHB (Gamma-hydroxybutyrate): GHB has been used as a general anesthetic with minimal side-effects in a limited safe dosage range. It was placed in Schedule I in March 2000 after widespread recreational use. Uniquely, this drug is also listed in Schedule III for limited uses, under the trademark Xyrem.

- 12-Methoxyibogamine (Ibogaine): Ibogaine has been used in opiate addiction treatment and psychotherapy.

- Cannabis (Tetrahydrocannabinol (THC) and substances containing THC): Controversy exists about its placement in Schedule I.

- Dimethyltryptamine (DMT), which is found in small quantities in the human brain but is pharmacologically active in larger quantities.

- Heroin (Diacetylmorphine), which is used in much of Europe as a potent pain reliever in terminal cancer patients. It is about twice as potent by weight as morphine.
- MDMA (3, 4-methylenedioxymethamphetamine, Ecstasy): Continues to be used medically, notably in the treatment of post-traumatic stress disorder (PTSD) (approved by the FDA for PTSD use in 2001).
- Psilocybin: The active ingredient in psychedelic mushrooms.
- Other strong opiates and opioids used in many other countries, or even in the USA in previous decades for palliation of moderate to severe pain include Vilan, Palfium, Ketalgin, Paramorfan, Dipidolor, Paralaudin, Wellconal, Heptalgin and many others. Weaker opioids include Peronine, Tusscodin, Thebacon, Valoron, Meptid, Algeril, acetyldihydrocodeine and others.

Schedule II drugs

The requirements to label a drug schedule II are as follows:
- The drug or other substance has a high potential for abuse.
- The drug or other substance has a currently accepted medical use in treatment in the United States or a currently accepted medical use with severe restrictions.
- Abuse of the drug or other substances may lead to severe psychological or physical dependence.

These drugs are only available by prescription, and distribution and production is carefully controlled and monitored by the DEA. Oral prescriptions are allowed, except that the prescription is limited to 30 days worth of doses, although exceptions are made for cancer patients, burn victims, etc. and oral prescriptions for schedule II drugs must be confirmed in writing within 3 days. No refills are allowed. The DEA is finalizing a Notice of Proposed Rulemaking in which it proposed to amend its regulations to allow practitioners to provide individual patients with multiple prescriptions, to be filled sequentially, for the same schedule II controlled substance, with such multiple prescriptions having the combined effect of allowing a patient to receive over time up to a 90-day supply of that controlled substance. Some of these drugs (notably Fentanyl in non-transdermal form) are never given to patients for home use, but are administered only by a physician. These drugs vary in potency: for example, Fentanyl is about 80 times as potent as morphine. (Heroin is only twice as potent.)

Below is a list of several schedule II drugs:
- Cocaine (used as a topical anesthetic)
- Methylphenidate (Ritalin) & Dexmethylphenidate (Focalin) (used in treatment of Attention Deficit Disorder)
- Opium
- Methadone (used in treatment of heroin addiction as well as for treatment of extreme chronic pain)
- Oxycodone (semi-synthetic opioid; active ingredient in Percocet, OxyContin, and Percodan)
- Morphine
- Amphetamine (racemic)
- Dextroamphetamine (Dexedrine)
- Dextromethamphetamine (Desoxyn)
- Hydromorphone (Dilaudid)
- Pure codeine and any drug for non-parenteral administration containing the equivalent of more than 90 mg of codeine per dosage unit.
- Pure hydrocodone and any drug for non-parenteral administration containing no other active ingredients or more than 15 mg per dosage unit
- Secobarbital (Seconal)
- Pethidine (USAN: Meperidine; Demerol)
- Phencyclidine (PCP)
- Most other pure strong opioid agonists (e.g., levorphanol, fentanyl, opium, or oxymorphone)

- Short-acting barbiturates, such as pentobarbital
- Amphetamines: Injectable methamphetamine has always been on Schedule II
- Nabilone (Cesamet) A synthetic cannabinoid. An analogue to dronabinol (Marinol) which is a Schedule III drug.

Schedule III drugs

The requirements to label a drug schedule III are as follows:
- The drug or other substance has a potential for abuse less than the drugs or other substances in schedules I and II.
- The drug or other substance has a currently accepted medical use in treatment in the United States.
- Abuse of the drug or other substance may lead to moderate or low physical dependence or high psychological dependence.

These drugs are available only by prescription, though control of wholesale distribution is somewhat less stringent than Schedule II drugs. Prescriptions for Schedule III drugs may be refilled up to five times within a six month period.

Below are descriptions of some schedule III drugs:
- Anabolic steroids (including prohormones such as androstenedione);
- Intermediate-acting barbiturates, such as talbutal or butalbital;
- Buprenorphine;
- Dihydrocodeine single-ingredient drugs and the pure drug itself.
- Ketamine, a drug originally developed as a milder substitute for PCP (mainly to use as a human anesthetic) but has since become popular as a veterinary and pediatric anesthetic;
- Xyrem, a preparation of GHB used to treat narcolepsy. Xyrem is in Schedule III but with a restricted distribution system. All other forms of GHB are in Schedule I;

- Hydrocodone / codeine, when compounded with an NSAID (e.g. Vicoprofen, when compounded with ibuprofen) or with acetaminophen (paracetamol) (e.g. Vicodin / Tylenol 3);

- Marinol, a synthetic form of Tetrahydrocannabinol (THC) used to treat nausea and vomiting caused by chemotherapy, as well as appetite loss caused by AIDS;

- Paregoric;

- LSA, listed as a sedative but considered by most experts to be psychedelic. A precursor to and chemical relative of LSD. LSA occurs naturally in Rivea corymbosa, morning glory seeds, and Hawaiian baby woodrose seeds.

Schedule IV drugs

The requirements to label a drug schedule IV are as follows:

- The drug or other substance has a low potential for abuse relative to the drugs or other substances in schedule III.

- The drug or other substance has a currently accepted medical use in treatment in the United States.

- Abuse of the drug or other substance may lead to limited physical dependence or psychological dependence relative to the drugs or other substances in schedule III.

Control measures are similar to Schedule III. Prescriptions for Schedule IV drugs may be refilled up to five times within a six month period.

Below are descriptions of several schedule IV drugs:

- Benzodiazepines, such as alprazolam (Xanax), chlordiazepoxide (Librium), diazepam (Valium), temazepam (Restoril), flunitrazepam (Rohypnol) (Note that Rohypnol is not used medically in the United States, and some states have placed it in Schedule I under state law.);

- The "Z-drugs": Zolpidem (Ambien), Zopiclone, Eszopiclone, and Zaleplon;

- Dextropropoxyphene (Doloxene) and propoxyphene (sold in the U.S. as Darvocet);
- Long-acting barbiturates such as phenobarbital;
- Some partial agonist opioid analgesics, such as pentazocine (Talwin);
- Phentermine;
- Certain non-amphetamine stimulants, including pemoline and the pseudostimulant modafinil.
- Chloral hydrate (sold as Aquachloral), used as a sedative and hypnotic.
- Meprobamate (Miltown)
- As listed on the US Customs web site under discussion of Khat, see cathine and its listing based on relative freshness.

Schedule V drugs

The requirements to label a drug schedule V are as follows:
- The drug or other substance has a low potential for abuse relative to the drugs or other substances in schedule IV.
- The drug or other substance has a currently accepted medical use in treatment in the United States.
- Abuse of the drug or other substance may lead to limited physical dependence or psychological dependence relative to the drugs or other substances in schedule IV.

Schedule V drugs are only available for a medical purpose.

Below are descriptions of some schedule V drugs:
- Cough suppressants containing small amounts of codeine (e.g., promethazine+codeine);
- Preparations containing small amounts of opium or diphenoxylate (used to treat diarrhea);
- Pregabalin (Lyrica), an anticonvulsant and pain modulator.

- Pyrovalerone
- The centrally-acting anti-diarrheals diphenoxylate (Lomotil) and difenoxin (Motofen) when mixed with atropine to make it unpleasant for people to grind up, cook, and shoot up. Otherwise the drugs are in Schedule II.

Schedule VI drugs

The federal law has only five schedules, but some states have added a "Schedule VI" to cover certain substances which are not "drugs" in the conventional sense, but are nonetheless used, or abused, recreationally; these include toluene (found in many types of paint, especially spray paint) and similar inhalants such as amyl nitrite (or "poppers"), butyl nitrite, and nitrous oxide (found in many types of aerosol cans, though it is pharmacologically active, it is considered an inhalant). Many state and local governments enforce age limits on the sale of products containing these substances.

Pharmaceuticals that require a prescription to be dispensed often are not covered under the Controlled Substances Act. This category includes medicines which should only be taken under a doctor's care, or which may have harmful interactions with other substances, but which are not known to be addictive and which are not used recreationally. These medications are used to treat a wide variety of medical conditions and to manage chronic conditions. Drugs requiring prescriptions are sometimes also known as legend drugs because legislation requires labels with the legend, "Caution! Federal law prohibits dispensing without a prescription." The term controlled drugs is sometimes used for scheduled drugs because of the additional controls placed on them (beyond the need for a prescription).

Paradox of drug placement

The placement of some drugs is paradoxical: both morphine and fentanyl are on Schedule II, and heroin is on Schedule I. Fentanyl is approximately 80 times the potency of morphine, and heroin is somewhere between morphine and fentanyl. Clearly, morphine has been used by physicians for over 150 years. It is very addictive, but it is very effective for severe pain, so it is licensed for careful medical use. Heroin was introduced in the late 19th century and licensed the same way until it was completely banned in 1924. Fentanyl has been used for less than 50 years and has always been carefully restricted. Dextromethorphan (DXM), a drug found in many OTC cough medications, is also explicitly exempt from scheduling under the original 1970 version of the CSA. However, the DEA has noted DXM to be abused recreationally as a dissociative anesthetic similar to PCP or ketamine. DXM is therefore listed as a 'chemical of concern' and is being considered for possible evaluation for scheduling.

Federal regulation of pseudoephedrine

Due to pseudoephedrine being widely used in the manufacture of methamphetamine, Congress passed the Methamphetamine Precursor Control Act which places restrictions on the sale of any medicine containing pseudoephedrine. That bill was then superseded by the Combat Methamphetamine Epidemic Act of 2005, which was passed as an amendment to the Patriot Act renewal and included wider and more comprehensive restrictions on the sale of pseudoephedrine containing products. This law requires customer signature of a "log-book" and presentation of valid photo ID to purchase of pseudoephedrine (PSE) containing products from all retailers.

The law restricts an individual to the retail sale of such products to no more than three packages or no more than nine grams in a single transaction. A violation of this statute constitutes a misdemeanor. In states where OTC medications which contain pseudoephedrine are not regulated, many retailers, notably Target and Wal-Mart have restricted their purchase by requiring it to be sold behind the pharmacy or service counter and/or placing an age restriction on purchase. Additionally, pharmacies such as CVS and Walgreens also require photo ID and log-book signatures for sales of PSE containing products in compliance with Federal law.

COX-2 inhibitors

These drugs have been derived from NSAIDs. The cyclooxygenase enzyme inhibited by NSAIDs was discovered to have at least 2 different versions: COX1 and COX2. Research suggested that most of the adverse effects of NSAIDs were mediated by blocking the COX1 (constitutive) enzyme, with the analgesic effects being mediated by the COX2 (inducible) enzyme. The COX2 inhibitors were thus developed to inhibit only the COX2 enzyme (traditional NSAIDs block both versions in general). These drugs (such as rofecoxib and celecoxib) are equally effective analgesics when compared with NSAIDs, but cause less gastrointestinal hemorrhage in particular. However, post-launch data indicated increased risk of cardiac and cerebrovascular events with these drugs due to an increased likelihood of clotting in the blood due to a decrease in the production of prostaglandin around the platelets causing less clotting factor to be released, and rofecoxib was subsequently withdrawn from the market. The role for this class of drug is currently hotly debated.

Pharmacological Principles

Pain management

Pain management generally benefits from a multidisciplinary approach that includes pharmacologic measures (analgesics such as narcotics or NSAIDs and pain modifiers such as tricyclic antidepressants or anticonvulsants), non-pharmacologic measures (such as interventional procedures, physical therapy and physical exercise, application of ice and/or heat), and psychological measures (such as biofeedback and cognitive therapy). Pain management practitioners come from all fields of medicine. Most often, pain fellowship trained physicians are anesthesiologists, neurologists, physiatrists or psychiatrists. Some practitioners focus more on the pharmacologic management of the patient, while others are very proficient at the interventional management of pain. Interventional procedures - typically used for chronic back pain - include: epidural steroid injections, facet joint injections, neurolytic blocks, Spinal Cord Stimulators and intrathecal drug delivery system implants, etc. Over the last several years the number of interventional procedures done for pain has grown to a very large number.

Drug interactions

There are four main ways in which drugs can interact. In an additive interaction, the cumulative effect of all the drugs taken is simply the sum total of the individual effects of each drug. In a synergistic interaction, however, the cumulative effect of all the drugs taken is greater than the effects of each individual drug. An example of a synergistic interaction is when barbiturates are mixed with alcohol, resulting in a greatly magnified depressant effect. A drug interaction is referred to as potentiating when one drug increases the effect of another. Alcohol, for example, has a potentiating effect on some cold medicines. Drugs are said to be antagonistic when they either neutralize or stifle the effects of one another.

Analgesics combined with other drugs

Analgesics are frequently used in combination, such as the paracetamol and codeine preparations found in many non-prescription pain relievers. They can also be found in combination with vasoconstrictor drugs such as pseudoephedrine for sinus-related preparations, or with antihistamine drugs for allergy sufferers.

The use of paracetamol, as well as aspirin, ibuprofen, naproxen, and other NSAIDS concurrently with weak to mid-range opiates (up to about the hydrocodone level) has been shown to have beneficial synergistic effects by combating pain at multiple sites of action—NSAIDs reduce inflammation which, in some cases, is the cause of the pain itself while opiates dull the perception of pain—thus, in cases of mild to moderate pain caused in part by inflammation, it is generally recommended that the two be prescribed together.

Acute effects of drug use

Acute (or recreational) drug use causes the release and prolonged action of dopamine and serotonin within the reward circuit. Different types of drug produce these effects by different methods. DA appears to harbor the largest effect and its action is characterized. DA binds to the D1 receptor, triggering a signaling cascade within the cell. cAMP-dependent protein kinase (PKA) phosphorylates cAMP response element binding protein (CREB), a transcription factor, which induces the synthesis of certain genes including C-Fos.

Bases of drug addiction

Reward circuit

The reward circuit, also known as the mesolimbic system, is a pathway in the brain by which one feels rewarded and due to which one may become addicted to such feelings of reward. It consists of the interaction of several areas of the brain; namely, the Ventral Tegmental Area (VTA) and the Nucleus Accumbens (NAc). The VTA consists of dopaminergic neurons which respond when stimuli indicative of a reward are present. This area supports learning and is responsible for sensitization and releases dopamine (DA) into the forebrain and the NAc through the mesolimbic pathway through which virtually all drugs causing drug addiction increase the release of dopamine. The Nucleus Accumbens is associated with acquiring and eliciting conditioned behaviors and thus is involved in conditioning the brain to repeat pleasurable acts, such as abuse of a drug, as it stimulates this pleasurable pathway. The prefrontal cortex, more specifically the anterior cingulate and orbitofrontal cortices, is important for the integration of information which contributes to whether a behavior will be elicited. It appears to be the area in which motivation originates and the salience of stimuli are determined. Also considered to be important for motivation is the basolateral amygdala, which projects into the NAc. More evidence is pointing towards the role of the hippocampus in drug addiction because of its importance in learning and memory.

Stress mechanisms

In addition to the reward circuit, it is hypothesized that stress mechanisms also play a role in addiction. Koob and Kreek have hypothesized that during drug use corticotropin-releasing factor (CRF) activates the hypothalamic-pituitary-adrenal axis (HPA) and other stress systems in the extended amygdala. This activation influences the deregulated emotional state associated with drug addiction. They have found that as drug use escalates, so does the presence of CRF in human cerebrospinal fluid (CSF). Other studies in this review showed a deregulation in other hormones associated with the HPA axis, including enkephalin, which is an endogenous opioid peptide that regulates pain. It also appears that the μ-opioid receptor system, which enkephalin acts on, is influential in the reward system and can regulate the expression of stress hormones.

Neuroplasticity in early drug use

Neuroplasticity is the putative mechanism behind learning and memory. It involves physical changes in the synapses between two communicating neurons, characterized by increased gene expression, altered cell signaling, and the formation of new synapses between the communicating neurons. When addictive drugs are present in the system, they appear to hijack this mechanism in the reward system so that motivation is geared towards procuring the drug rather than natural rewards. Depending on the history of drug use, nucleus accumbens (NAc) excitatory synapses experience two types of neuroplasticity, or bidirectional plasticity, long-term potentiation (LTP) and long-term depression (LTD). It has been displayed that chronic exposure to cocaine increases the strength of synapses in NAc after a 10-14 day withdrawal period, while strengthened synapses did not appear within a 24 hour withdrawal period after repeated cocaine exposure. A single dose of cocaine did not display any attributes of a strengthened synapse. When drug experienced subjects were challenged with one dose of cocaine, synaptic depression occurred. Therefore, it seems the history of cocaine exposure along with withdrawal times affects the direction of glutamatergic plasticity in the NAc

Decreased neurogenesis

Drug addiction also raises the issue of potential harmful effects on the development of new neurons in adults. Eisch and Harburg raise three new concepts they have extrapolated from the numerous recent studies on drug addiction. First, neurogenesis decreases as a result of repeated exposure to additive drugs. A list of studies show that chronic use of opiates, psychostimulants, nicotine, and alcohol decrease neurogenesis. Second, this apparent decrease in neurogenesis seems to be independent of HPA axis activation. Other environmental factors other than drug exposure such as age, stress and exercise, can also have an effect of neurogenesis by regulating the hypothalamic-pituitary-adrenal (HPA) axis. Mounting evidence suggests this for 3 reasons: small doses of opiates and psychostimulants increase corticosterone concentration in serum but with no effect of neurogenesis; although decreased neurogenesis is similar between self-administered and forced drug intake, activation of HPA axis is greater in self-administration subjects; and even after the inhibition of opiate induced increase of corticosterone, a decrease in neurogenesis occurred. Last, addictive drugs appear to only affect proliferation in the subgranular zone (SGZ), rather than other areas associated with neurogenesis. The studies of drug use and neurogenesis may have implications on stem cell biology

Drug sensitization

Sensitization is the increase in sensitivity to a drug after prolonged use. The proteins delta FosB and regulator of G-protein Signaling 9-2 (RGS 9-2) are thought to be involved:

A transcription factor, known as delta FosB, is thought to activate genes that, counter to the effects of CREB, actually increase the user's sensitivity to the effects of the substance. Delta FosB slowly builds up with each exposure to the drug and remains activated for weeks after the last exposure—long after the effects of CREB have faded. The hypersensitivity that it causes is thought to be responsible for the intense cravings associated with drug addiction, and is often extended to even the peripheral cues of drug use, such as related behaviors or the sight of drug paraphernalia. There is some evidence that delta FosB even causes structural changes within the nucleus accumbens, which presumably helps to perpetuate the cravings, and may be responsible for the high incidence of relapse that occur in treated drug addicts.

In studies animals lacking RGS 9-2 appear to have increased sensitivity to dopamine receptor agonists such as cocaine and amphetamines; over-expression of RGS 9-2 causes a lack of responsiveness to these same agonists.

Psychological drug tolerance

The reward system is partly responsible for the psychological part of drug tolerance; The CREB protein, a transcription factor activated by cyclic adenosine monophosphate (cAMP) immediately after a high, triggers genes that produce proteins such as dynorphin, which cuts off dopamine release and temporarily inhibits the reward circuit. In chronic drug users, a sustained activation of CREB thus forces a larger dose to be taken to reach the same effect. In addition it leaves the user feeling generally depressed and dissatisfied, and unable to find pleasure in previously enjoyable activities, often leading to a return to the drug for an additional "fix".

Mechanisms of effect

Depressants

Depressants such as alcohol and benzodiazepines work by increasing the affinity of the GABA receptor for its ligand; GABA. Narcotics such as morphine and methadone, work by mimicking endorphins—chemicals produced naturally by the body which have effects similar to dopamine—or by disabling the neurons that normally inhibit the release of dopamine in the reward system. These substances (sometimes called "downers") typically facilitate relaxation and pain-relief.

<u>Stimulants</u>

Stimulants such as amphetamines, nicotine, and cocaine, increase dopamine signaling in the reward system either by directly stimulating its release, or by blocking its absorption. These substances (sometimes called "uppers") typically cause heightened alertness and energy. They cause a pleasant feeling in the body, and euphoria, known as a high. This high wears off leaving the user feeling depressed. This makes them want more of the drug, worsening the addiction.

Drug metabolism

Drug metabolism is the metabolism of drugs, their biochemical modification or degradation, usually through specialized enzymatic systems. This is a form of xenobiotic metabolism. Drug metabolism often converts lipophilic chemical compounds into more readily excreted polar products. Its rate is an important determinant of the duration and intensity of the pharmacological action of drugs. Drug metabolism can result in toxication or detoxication - the activation or deactivation of the chemical. While both occur, the major metabolites of most drugs are detoxication products.

Drugs are almost all xenobiotics. Other commonly used organic chemicals are also drugs, and are metabolized by the same enzymes as drugs. This provides the opportunity for drug-drug and drug-chemical interactions or reactions.

<u>Differences of age and sex</u>

Increased susceptibility to the pharmacologic or toxic activity of drugs has been reported in very young and old patients as compared to young adults. Although this may reflect differences in absorption, distribution, and elimination, differences in drug metabolism cannot be ruled out. Studies in several mammalian species indicate that drugs are metabolized at reduced rates during the prepubertal period and senescence. Slower metabolism could be due to reduced activity of metabolic enzymes or reduced availability of essential endogenous cofactors.

Sex-dependent variations in drug metabolism have been well documented in rats but not in other rodents. Young adult male rats metabolize drugs much faster than mature female rats or prepubertal male rats. These differences in drug metabolism have been clearly associated with androgenic hormones. A few clinical reports suggest that similar sex-dependent differences in drug metabolism also exist in other animals for benzodiazepines, estrogens, and salicylates.

Route of administration

In pharmacology and toxicology, a route of administration is the path by which a drug, fluid, poison or other substance is brought into contact with the body. Obviously, a substance must be transported from the site of entry to the part of the body where its action is desired to take place (even if this only means penetration through the stratum corneum into the skin). However, using the body's transport mechanisms for this purpose can be far from trivial. The pharmacokinetic properties of a drug (that is, those related to processes of uptake, distribution, and elimination) are critically influenced by the route of administration.

Enteral routes
Enteral is any form of administration that involves any part of the gastrointestinal tract:
- by mouth (orally), many drugs as tablets, capsules, or drops
- by gastric feeding tube, duodenal feeding tube, or gastrostomy, many drugs and enteral nutrition
- rectally, various drugs in suppository or enema form

Topical routes
- epicutaneous (application onto the skin), e.g. allergy testing, typical local anesthesia
- inhalational, e.g. asthma medications

- enema, e.g. contrast media for imaging of the bowel
- eye drops (onto the conjunctiva), e.g. antibiotics for conjunctivitis
- ear drops - such as antibiotics and corticosteroids for otitis externa
- intranasal route (into the nose), e.g. decongestant nasal sprays
- vaginal, e.g. topical estrogens, antibacterials

<u>Parenteral routes</u>

- transdermal (diffusion through the intact skin), e.g. transdermal opioid patches in pain therapy, nicotine patches for treatment of addiction
  - transmucosal (diffusion through a mucous membrane), e.g. insufflation (snorting) of cocaine, sublingual nitroglycerine, buccal (absorbed through cheek near gumline)
  - inhalational, e.g. inhalational anesthetics
  - intravenous (into a vein), e.g. many drugs, total parenteral nutrition
  - intraarterial (into an artery), e.g. vasodilator drugs in the treatment of vasospasm and thrombolytic drugs for treatment of embolism
  - intramuscular (into a muscle), e.g. many vaccines, antibiotics, and long-term psychoactive agents
  - intracardiac (into the heart), e.g. adrenaline during cardiopulmonary resuscitation (no longer commonly performed)
  - subcutaneous (under the skin), e.g. insulin
  - intraosseous infusion (into the bone marrow) is, in effect, an indirect intravenous access because the bone marrow drains directly into the venous system. This route is occasionally used for drugs and fluids in emergency medicine and pediatrics when intravenous access is difficult.
  - intradermal, (into the skin itself) is used for skin testing some allergens, and also for tattoos
  - intrathecal (into the spinal canal) is most commonly used for spinal anesthesia and chemotherapy

- intraperitoneal, (infusion or injection into the peritoneum) e.g. peritoneal dialysis is predominantly used in veterinary medicine and animal testing for the administration of systemic drugs and fluids due to the ease of administration compared with other parenteral methods

Dose response curve

A dose-response curve is a simple X-Y graph relating the magnitude of a stressor (e.g. concentration of a pollutant, amount of a drug, temperature, intensity of radiation) to the response of the receptor (e.g. organism under study). The response is usually death (mortality), but other effects (or endpoints) can be studied. The measured dose (usually in milligrams, micrograms, or grams per kilogram of body-weight) is generally plotted on the X axis and the response is plotted on the Y axis. Commonly, it is the logarithm of the dose that is plotted on the X axis, and in such cases the curve is typically sigmoidal, with the steepest portion in the middle. The first point along the graph where a response above zero is reached is usually referred to as a threshold-dose. For most beneficial or recreational drugs, the desired effects are found at doses slightly greater than the threshold dose. At higher doses still, undesired side effects appear and grow stronger as the dose increases. The stronger a particular substance is, the steeper this curve will be. In quantitative situations, the Y-axis usually is designated by percentages, which refer to the percentage of users registering a standard response (which is often death, when the 50% mark refers to LD50). Such a curve is referred to as a quantal dose response curve, distinguishing it from a graded dose response curve, where response is continuous.

Initial effects on the brain

Initially, drugs dramatically affect the brain reward circuitry, causing molecular changes that can last for months, and even forever. Research shows that the drug-induced biochemical and structural redesign of the brain starts from the first experience with a drug. Continued drug use recruits and redesigns more areas of the brain via neurochemical sensitization. More specifically, when drug use continues, the glutamate-mediated drug seeking system will gradually take over the command from the dopamine-mediated brain reward system. The changes in brain structure and function predominantly occur in areas involved in sophisticated reasoning as well as in areas responsible for day to day survival. Frighteningly, these changes are beyond the reach of will power and beyond the reach of psychological insight.

All the drugs that people abuse have one action in common. Initially, drugs change the way the limbic system works in a specific limbic circuit that generates feelings of pleasure, which is called the brain reward circuitry. More specifically, all psychoactive substances share the common property of increasing dramatically dopamine levels in the Nucleus Accumbens. Drugs hijack the brain's survival system!!

Reorganization of neural circuitry

The three general principles in the reorganization of neural circuitry are:

- A final common pathway-the glutamatergic projection from the prefrontal cortex to the Nucleus Accumbens to the ventral pallidum is a final common pathway for drug seeking initiated by stress, a drug-associated cue or the drug itself. This means an increased release of glutamate in the Nuc. Accumbens and in the Ventral Pallidum.

- Different modes of stimuli involve distinct components of the circuit. Notice the involvement of the amygdala (that belongs to the limbic system): cue-primed drug seeking requires involvement of the basolateral amygdala, while stress- and drug-primed drug seeking do not.

- Drug-seeking stimuli require dopamine transmission while the rewarding effects that accompany drug use depend on increased dopamine release in the Nuc. Accumbens, the reinstatement of drug seeking requires dopamine

- 63 -

release in the prefrontal cortex and in the amygdala, not in the Nuc. Accumbens.

Neuroplasticity after transition to addiction

Once a person has transitioned from drug use to addiction, behavior becomes completely geared towards seeking the drug, even though addicts report the euphoria is not as intense as it once was. Despite the differing actions of drugs during acute use, the final pathway of addiction is the same. Another aspect of drug addiction is a decreased response to normal biological stimuli, such as food, sex, and social interaction. Through functional brain imaging of patients addicted to cocaine, scientists have been able to visualize increased metabolic activity in the anterior cingulate and orbitofrontal cortex, areas of the brain in addicted subjects involved in the more intense motivation to find the drug rather than seeking natural rewards, as well as an addict's decreased ability to overcome this urge. Imaging has also shown cocaine-addicted subjects to have decreased activity in their prefrontal cortex when presented with stimuli associated with natural rewards. The transition from recreational drug use to addiction occurs in gradual stages and is produced by the effect of a drug on the neuroplasticity of the neurons found in the reward circuit. During events preceding addiction, cravings are produced by the release of dopamine (DA) in the prefrontal cortex. As a person transitions from drug use to addiction, the release of DA in the NAc becomes unnecessary to produce cravings; rather, DA transmission decreases while increased metabolic activity in the orbitofrontal cortex contributes to cravings. Early this neurometamorphosis is reversible, but becomes permanent with extended exposure.

Mechanisms behind effect on synaptic plasticity

The exact mechanism behind a drug molecule's effect on synaptic plasticity is still unclear. However, neuroplasticity in glutamatergic projections seems to be a major result of repeated drug exposure. There are several ways in which glutamate transmission is altered. One way is by increasing presynaptic release of glutamate and the other is increased response to glutamate. The two main glutamate receptors involved are NMDAR and AMPAR. The expression of these receptors on the cell surface increases with repeated drug use. This type of synaptic plasticity results in LTP, which strengthens connections between two neurons; onset of this occurs quickly and the result is constant. In addition to glutamatergic neurons, dopaminergic neurons present in the VTA respond to glutamate and may be recruited earliest during neural adaptations caused by repeated drug exposure. As shown by Kourrich, et al., one's history of drug exposure and the time of withdrawal from last exposure appear to play an important role in the direction of plasticity in the neurons of the reward system.

An aspect of neuron development that may also play a part in drug-induced neuroplasticity is the presence of axon guidance molecules such as semaphorins and ephrins. After repeated cocaine treatment, altered expression (increase or decrease dependent on the type of molecule) of mRNA coding for axon guidance molecules occurred in rats. This may contribute to the alterations in the reward circuit characteristic of drug addiction.

Effects of drugs on neuron communication

Drugs work in the brain because they have a similar size and shape as natural neurotransmitters (NTs) and interact with receptors and other components of the synapse. Drugs masquerade as NTs and therefore interfere with normal synaptic transmission by introducing false messages or by changing the strength of real ones. Disrupting the transmission of information at the synapse is the basic mechanism by which drugs change behavior. Drugs lock into receptors and start an unnatural chain reaction of electrical charges, causing neurons to release large amounts of their own NT. Much more dopamine is released, thus there is increased activation of dopamine receptors. This causes increased production of the intracellular second messenger Cyclic AMP inside the post-synaptic cell which alters the normal activity of the neuron. Through upregulation of Cyclic AMP, drugs induce a variety of molecular changes in neurons, thereby remodeling and restructuring neurons. Synaptic plasticity by psychoactive substances can occur via changes in NT release, the status of the NT receptors, receptor-mediated signaling or the number of ion channels regulating neuronal excitability. Repeated stimulation of receptors by drugs can lead to alterations in receptor number and function. There are both presynaptic changes (increased dopamine release) and postsynaptic changes (changes in receptor sensitivity).The result of this process is that drugs change the way the brain works and thus how people perceive the world, feel about themselves, and how they behave.

Activation of VTA neurons by drugs

When a drug activates the VTA neurons, they release huge amounts of dopamine into synapses within the Nucleus Accumbens. The brain becomes flooded with dopamine. When this happens, drug users feel immense pleasure. Dependence-producing drugs differ from conventional reinforcers in that their stimulant effect on dopamine release in the Nucleus Accumbens is significantly greater than natural reinforcers such as food. Illegal drugs activate the brain reward system with a potency that natural rewards can rarely match. Because of the effect of drugs on the brain reward system, the brain of the drug user believes that drugs are essential for the drug users' survival. It is literally a hijacking of the brain's survival systems, confusing day to day survival with the need for more drugs. The brain has powerful feedback systems to say "enough" when it comes to natural behaviors, such as feeding and sex. But there is no natural feedback loop in the brain turning off the effects of drugs on the brain reward system. Due to adaptive alterations in the brain reward circuitry, drug addicts may no longer be able to feel the benefits of natural rewards (food, water, sex) or function normally without the drug present. Addictive substances thus hijack the brain's survival system, weakening one's resolve to make wise choices even when painful consequences are sure to result. Addicts do not act like rational humans because drugs also change the role of the cerebral cortex, the very brain region that gives us our ability to evaluate a variety of contingencies and make reasoned choices.

Neurobiological basis of drug conditioning

The release of dopamine acts as a signal to initiate adaptive behavioral responses to the motivational event (drug use or drug-associated cues). The release of dopamine facilitates cellular changes that establish learned associations with drug use. In this way the organism can more effectively emit an adaptive behavioral response should the event reoccur. Dopamine has 2 functions in the brain: to alert the organism to the appearance of important stimuli, thereby promoting neuroplasticity (learning), and to alert the organism to the pending appearance of a familiar motivationally relevant event (such as drug use), on the basis of learned associations made with environmental stimuli predicting the event. Conditioned stimuli continue to trigger release of dopamine. The amygdala (that belongs to the limbic system) is especially critical in establishing learned associations between motivationally relevant events and otherwise neutral stimuli that become predictors of the event (drug use). The anterior cingulated and ventral orbital cortices in the prefrontal cortex are recruited by motivationally relevant events, as well as stimuli that predict such events, and contribute to whether a behavioral response will be emitted, as well as the intensity of that response. It needs to be stressed that the involvement of the Nucleus Accumbens in expressing adaptive behaviors depends mainly on glutamatergic projections from the prefrontal cortex. The increase of the neurotransmitter glutamate is essentially a "go" signal. It urges the individual to act.

Drug administration

Drugs can be introduced to the body through different means. The most common way of taking a drug is by oral administration, i.e., swallowing it in a solid, liquid, or plasma form. Drugs may be injected directly into the bloodstream, a method that produces faster results than oral administration. Drugs may be inhaled; inhalants that are placed in a plastic bag and breathed are said to be huffed. There are different types of injections: intravenous injections are made directly into a vein; intramuscular injections are made into muscle tissue; and subcutaneous injections are made below the skin. Of these, intravenous injection is the fastest acting, while the effects of a subcutaneous injection may not be felt for 10 minutes or more.

Drug toxicity and ways of action

The toxicity level of a drug is the administered amount that will be poisonous to the body. A drug taken at a toxic level will cause either temporary or permanent damage to the body. Indeed, the enzymes in the liver that are responsible for breaking down drugs are called detoxification enzymes. Drugs may act locally, generally, or selectively. A drug acts locally when it only affects a specific area of the body. A drug acts generally when it affects an entire system of the body. A barbiturate, for instance, has a deadening effect on the entire nervous system. A drug acts selectively when it has a much greater effect on one organ or system than any other. Some anesthetics, for instance, will numb an isolated part of the body. .

Biology of drug addiction

Recently, scientists have made great progress in understanding the biology of addiction by observing that many of the substances involved (alcohol, marijuana, and cocaine, for instance) trigger the release of dopamine in the brain. Dopamine is a neurotransmitter associated with feelings of satisfaction and pleasure. Not only do many addictive substances raise the level of dopamine in the brain, they also alter the pathways through which dopamine is released and accessed in the brain. Because of this alteration, the user comes to experience satisfaction and pleasure only when the particular addictive substance is being used. There is also evidence to suggest that individuals born with especially low levels of dopamine may be more susceptible to drug addiction.

Alcohol and Tobacco

One alcoholic drink

Any liquid that contains sugar and is fermented will produce the colorless liquid known as alcohol. The kind of alcohol found in alcoholic beverages is ethyl alcohol. Since different alcoholic beverages contain different amounts of alcohol, a standard measurement for one drink has been created. In health literature, a single drink may be 12 ounces of beer (assumed to be 5% alcohol), 4 ounces of table wine (12% alcohol), 2.5 ounces of fortified wine (20%), or one ounce of distilled spirits (50% alcohol). Each of these drinks contains approximately half an ounce of ethyl alcohol. The amount of alcohol may also be measured in terms of proof, which is derived by multiplying the percentage of alcohol by 2. Thus, a bottle of whiskey that is 40% alcohol will be marked as 80 proof.

BAC

In order to figure out what amount of alcohol a person may consume at a time, it is important to determine their blood-alcohol concentration. BAC is the measure taken by breath or urine samples, including those administered to drivers suspected of being under the influence. According to the Federal Department of Transportation, a person should be considered unfit to drive if he or she has a BAC of 0.08% or higher. This is approximately the BAC that a 150-pound man will have after consuming three drinks in an hour. A BAC of 0.05% or higher will cause a person to experience many of the problems associated with intoxication; a BAC of 0.2% will probably result in the person losing consciousness; a BAC of 0.3% can result in a coma; and a BAC of 0.4% generally means death.

The effects of alcohol intoxication are greatly influenced by individual variations; some users may become intoxicated at a much lower BAC level than others. Some effects of alcohol at specific BAC levels are described below:

- 0.02-0.03: No loss of coordination, slight euphoria and loss of shyness. Mildly relaxed and perhaps a little lightheaded.

- 0.04-0.06: Feeling of well-being, relaxation, lower inhibitions, sensation of warmth. Euphoria. Some minor impairment of reasoning and memory, lowering of caution. Intensified emotions.

- 0.07-0.09: Slight impairment of balance, speech, vision, reaction time, and hearing. Euphoria. Judgment and self-control are reduced, and caution, reason and memory are impaired.

- 0.10-0.125: Significant impairment of motor coordination and loss of good judgment. Speech may be slurred; balance, vision, reaction time and hearing will be impaired. Euphoria. It is illegal to operate a motor vehicle at this level of intoxication in all states.

- 0.13-0.15: Dysphoria begins to appear, while one experiences gross motor impairment along with poor judgment and perception.

- 0.16-0.19: Dysphoria predominates, nausea may appear. The drinker has the appearance of a "sloppy drunk."

- 0.20: Feeling dazed/confused or otherwise disoriented. May need help to stand/walk. Pain threshold very high. Nausea, vomiting and blackouts are likely at this level.

- 0.25: All mental, physical and sensory functions are severely impaired. Increased risk of asphyxiation from choking on vomit and being seriously injured.

- 0.30: Stupor. One has little comprehension of where one is. One may pass out suddenly and be difficult to awaken.

- 0.35: Coma is possible. This is the level of surgical anesthesia.

- 0.40: Onset of coma, and possible death due to respiratory arrest.

BAL

The amount of alcohol in your blood stream is referred to as Blood Alcohol Level (BAL). It is recorded in milligrams of alcohol per 100 milliliters of blood, or milligrams percent. For example, a BAL of .10 means that 1/10 of 1 percent (or 1/1000) of your total blood content is alcohol. When you drink alcohol it goes directly from the stomach into the blood stream. This is why you typically feel the effects of alcohol quite quickly, especially if you haven't eaten in a while.
BAL depends on: 1. Amount of blood (which will increase with weight) and 2. The amount of alcohol you consume over time (the faster you drink, the higher your BAL, as the liver can only handle about a drink per hour--the rest builds up in your blood stream).

The effects of an increasing BAL are as follows:
- .02 MELLOW FEELING. SLIGHT BODY WARMTH. LESS INHIBITED.
- .05 NOTICEABLE RELAXATION. LESS ALERT. LESS SELF-FOCUSED. COORDINATION IMPAIRMENT BEGINS.
- .08 DRUNK DRIVING LIMIT. DEFINITE IMPAIRMENT IN COORDINATION AND JUDGMENT.
- .10 NOISY. POSSIBLE EMBARRASSING BEHAVIOR. MOOD SWINGS. REDUCTION IN REACTION TIME.
- .15 IMPAIRED BALANCE AND MOVEMENT. CLEARLY DRUNK.
- .30 MANY LOSE CONSCIOUSNESS
- .40 MOST LOSE CONSCIOUSNESS; SOME DIE.
- .50 BREATHING STOPS. MANY DIE.

As can be seen, the most reliably pleasurable effects of alcohol occur when BAL rises to about .03-.05. Alcohol researchers have discovered that low levels of alcohol have a specific effect on thinking; alcohol results in a reduction of "self-monitoring." What this means is that small quantities of alcohol enable you to take your mind off yourself and your worries. This effect reduces tension and enhances relaxation in many people. Some people find this effect so rewarding that they continue to drink. Unfortunately, the effect on self monitoring diminishes as BAL rises above .05. Instead emerge a host of negative effects, such as less emotional control, coordination and judgment impairment, hangovers and obnoxious behavior.

Misconceptions

"If I have too much to drink, I can drink a lot of coffee to sober up quickly. Right?" Drinking a lot of coffee after drinking too much alcohol may, however, increase your discomfort through the need to use the bathroom while being transported to the jail on DUI charges. Only time reverses impairment.

"Will eating breath mints after drinking fool a police 'breath test'?"

Eating mints will not affect your BAC level since it isn't the smell of your breath, but the alcohol content, that's measured.

"Well, at least eating breath mints might fool the officer, right?"

Get real.

"If I eat a BIG meal before drinking, won't that help keep me from getting drunk?" How much you have eaten, and how recently, may have a small effect on how quickly or slowly the alcohol you consume will enter your bloodstream — but it won't stop the alcohol from entering. If you drink too much, you will become intoxicated.

"Will splashing cold water on my face or taking a cold shower help sober me up?"

Nope, Splash away!

"Will running around the block a few times sober me up enough to drive home?"

Exercise won't sober you up any faster.

Nothing sobers up a drinker except time.

Recommended levels of consumption

Alcohol is not entirely bad for the body; in fact, there is consistent evidence that suggests a single drink every day can reduce an individual's risk of heart disease. This is truer for men than for women. The National Institute of Alcohol and Alcohol Abuse suggests that men should have no more than two drinks every day, and women should have no more than one. This amount should be adjusted, depending on an individual's weight or age. Many individuals, including pregnant women, people with ulcers, people on certain prescription medications, or those operating heavy machinery, shouldn't drink at all. The health risks associated with alcohol increase in proportion to the amount of alcohol that is consumed.

Individual response to alcohol

Several things determine the severity of an individual's response to alcohol. Obviously, the more alcohol consumed, the higher the individual's blood-alcohol concentration will be. Also, since the liver can only process half an ounce of alcohol every hour, heavy drinking results in a higher level of intoxication than moderate drinking. More potent forms of alcohol, like liquor and fortified wine, get into the bloodstream more quickly than less concentrated beverages, like beer, especially if the liquor is accompanied by a carbonated beverage. Heavy individuals tend to get drunk more slowly as they have an excess of water with which to dilute the incoming alcohol. Typically, women tolerate alcohol less well than men because they have less of the stomach enzyme that neutralizes alcohol. Older individuals tend to have less water and so are more affected by alcohol. The effects of alcohol are seen more quickly if it is taken on an empty stomach, if tolerance to it has not been built up, or if it is accompanied by a prescription medication.

Effects of alcohol

Immediate effects

From the moment it is consumed, and even before the individual notices any of the psychological effects, alcohol is at work in the human body. It is almost immediately absorbed into the bloodstream through the walls of the stomach and the upper intestine. Typically, it takes about 15 minutes for the alcohol in a drink to reach the bloodstream and, usually, about 1 hour for the alcohol to reach its peak. Once in the bloodstream, alcohol is carried to the liver, heart, and brain. Although alcohol cannot leave the body until it is metabolized by the liver, it is a diuretic that accelerates the removal of other liquids from the body; thus, alcohol has a dehydrating effect. Alcohol also lowers the temperature of the body.

Digestive system

The first stop for alcohol is the stomach. It is partially broken down there, and the remainder of it is absorbed into the bloodstream through the stomach lining. While in the stomach, alcohol stimulates the release of certain chemicals that tend to irritate the lining; it is for this reason that heavy drinking often causes nausea and chronic drinking may contribute to ulcers. The alcohol in the bloodstream moves on to the liver where, for the most part, it will be converted into fat. If an individual consumes four or five drinks a day for a few weeks, the liver cells will accrue a large amount of fat. Heavy alcohol use may eventually cause white blood cells to attack the liver, which can cause irreparable damage.

Cardiovascular and immune systems

Alcohol is thought to have some positive effects on the cardiovascular system. Light drinkers seem to have healthier hearts, fewer heart attacks, lower cholesterol levels, and, thus, a lower risk for heart disease than those who abstain altogether. In contrast, excessive drinking will weaken the heart muscle, and this is particularly true if alcohol is used in combination with tobacco and cocaine. Chronic alcohol use will inhibit the creation of white blood cells (which help fight infection) and of red blood cells (which carry oxygen around the body). It is dangerous for a person suffering from an infection (like a cold or the flu), to drink alcohol because it will suppress the immune system's ability to fight the infection.

Brain

When consumed in low volume, alcohol alters the areas of the brain that influence behavior in a way that makes the individual feel more relaxed and less inhibited. Of course, this is accompanied by deficits in concentration, memory, judgment, and motor control. Heavy drinkers may experience long-term intelligence and memory impairment. This occurs because alcohol depresses the central nervous system and slows down the activity of the neurons in the brain. This dulling of mental reactions increases in proportion to the amount of alcohol consumed and can culminate in unconsciousness, coma, or even death. Although one or two drinks may have a pleasant tranquilizing effect, many more can entirely snuff out central nervous system activity.

Behavior and judgment

Alcohol has a number of effects on behavior and judgment. It is known to impair sensory perceptions: the eye is less able to adjust to bright lights, and the ear has difficulty distinguishing sounds. The senses of smell and taste are also diminished by excessive consumption of alcohol. Alcohol will decrease sensitivity in general, making it possible for individuals to feel comfortable in extreme temperatures that may be hazardous to their health. Intoxication typically causes an impairment of motor skills, meaning that activities performed with the muscles cannot be done with any precision or coordination. Intoxication usually has a negative effect on sexual performance, even though it may increase interest in sexual activity.

Alcohol intoxication

The immediate consequence of alcohol consumption is intoxication. Individuals who become intoxicated from alcohol will exhibit negative behavioral and psychological changes, which may include aggressive behavior, inappropriate sexual conduct, mood changes, and impaired judgment. In addition, intoxication is generally manifested by the following: slurred speech, poor coordination, unsteady walking, abnormal eye movements, impaired concentration and memory, and a general stupor. Severe intoxication may cause a loss of concentration, coma, and even death. Intoxicated individuals are also at greater risk of infection because alcohol suppresses the work of the immune system. Severely intoxicated individuals may be at risk of shock if they lose consciousness.

Alcohol combined with drugs

The dangers of alcohol may be magnified greatly if it is consumed in combination with other drugs, whether legal or illegal. Indeed, more than half the most frequently prescribed drugs contain one or more ingredients that react with alcohol. In most cases, this is because the ingredient affects the same areas of the brain as alcohol, thus increasing the pharmacological effects. Particularly, the synergistic combination of alcohol and an antidepressant or antianxiety medication can be fatal. One commonly used drug that is thought to have negative consequences when taken with alcohol is aspirin. Although many people take aspirin to alleviate the negative consequences of drinking, research has shown that aspirin may diminish the stomach's ability to process alcohol.

Alcohol-related death

Alcohol can kill those who abuse it in various ways. The main cause of death is injury, generally sustained in auto accidents involving drunk driving. In fact, alcohol is involved in at least half of all traffic fatalities (as well as being involved in half of all homicides and a quarter of all suicides). After injury, the second most common cause of death related to alcohol is cirrhosis of the liver and other digestive disease. Health professionals believe that about half the people admitted to the hospital have a health problem related to alcohol. As would be expected, young drinkers are more likely to die from injury and older drinkers more likely to succumb to alcohol-related illness.

Reasons for drinking

Alcohol has been popular throughout history because it depresses the central nervous system and makes people feel more relaxed. People also often drink in celebration or when meeting with friends because alcohol tends to reduce inhibitions and make conversation easier. People who drink alcohol often report feeling smarter, sexier, or stronger, even if studies indicate the opposite. Alcohol is also used by many people as a way to escape personal problems or a bad mood. It is also true that many people drink because they are swayed by the massive advertising campaigns launched by brewers; indeed, the effects of alcohol advertising on underage consumers remain a controversial topic. Finally, many people drink in order to emulate people they admire, whether celebrities, family members, or peers.

Light, infrequent, moderate, and social drinking

Though there are no set standards for the varying degrees of alcohol consumption, there are a few basic patterns of drinking that are agreed upon by health professionals. Light drinking is usually defined as having three or fewer alcoholic beverages every week. Infrequent drinking is having less than one drink a month, but more than one drink in a year. Infrequent drinkers can often be those who rarely drink but, on the occasions when they do, are apt to drink four or more drinks. A moderate drinker is one who has approximately 12 drinks a week but is not impaired in any life domain. Social drinking is not defined by a particular quantity; rather, it is drinking at a level consistent with one's peer group, whether this level is high or low.

Problem and binge drinking

The individuals who are at great risk of developing health problems from alcohol are those who follow the patterns known as problem drinking and binge drinking. Problem drinking is defined as any amount of drinking that interferes with a major part of the individual's life, whether safety, sleep, energy, family relationships, sexual activity, or health. Although some of the negative consequences associated with problem drinking are immediate (like bad judgment and physical impairment), other effects of consistent alcohol abuse may be evident only over the long term. Binge drinking is defined for a man as having five or more drinks in a sitting (the amount is four for a woman). Binge drinking is most common among young, single men.

Female alcoholism

Even though women are less likely to abuse alcohol than men, many women still drink too much. Furthermore, women tend to drink for different reasons than men. Many women have an increased susceptibility to alcohol written into their genes. Female alcoholics are more likely than male alcoholics to have a parent who drinks heavily, has psychiatric problems, or has attempted suicide. Approximately 25% of female alcoholics report that they were physically or sexually abused during childhood. Women are more likely than men to be depressed before and during a period of alcoholism. Women who are single, separated, or divorced tend to drink more than married women, though women who cohabitate with a man without being married are the most likely to be problem drinkers. Women tend to drink more when they lose a social role, e.g., when their children grow up and leave, they lose their job, or they are divorced.

Health

Besides the obvious risks of alcohol as regards sexual behavior and driving, women face a number of health consequences for chronic alcoholism. Women take alcohol into the bloodstream more easily than men and are, thus, more likely to suffer liver damage from overwhelming amounts of alcohol than are men. Moderate and heavy drinking may also contribute to infertility, menstrual problems, sexual dysfunction, and premenstrual syndrome. If a woman drinks during pregnancy, her child may develop fetal alcohol syndrome: the child will be born with a small head, abnormal facial features, and possible intellectual disabilities. Other babies of drinking mothers may be underweight or irritable as newborns. Female alcoholics are at greater risk for breast cancer, osteoporosis, and heart disease.

Treatment

Unfortunately, female alcoholics do not always receive the same quality of care and social support as male alcoholics. Often, this is because of women have lower incomes than men or because women are burdened with the responsibilities of raising children. Studies have also shown that women are more likely to blame their personal problems on anxiety or depression, whereas men more readily admit to a drinking problem. Female alcoholics are more likely to become addicted to prescription medications or to develop eating disorders and sexual dysfunctions. Many health professionals believe targeting the causes of female alcoholism, like low self-esteem and depression, is a promising approach to treatment. Other organizations, like Women for Sobriety, are working to ensure that female alcoholism is recognized as a serious problem that demands attention.

Alcohol abuse

Alcohol abuse is defined by the American Psychiatric Association as the continued use of alcohol despite an awareness of the persistent social, physical, psychological, or professional problems it is causing. Alcohol abusers frequently consume alcohol at inappropriate times or in dangerous situations, like at work or before driving. An individual who is diagnosed as an alcohol abuser usually has trouble fulfilling a major role at work, school, or home and may have legal problems related to alcohol use.

Alcohol dependence

Alcohol dependence is differentiated from alcohol abuse by the following three factors: it involves the development of a physical craving for alcohol, a gradually increasing tolerance of the effects of alcohol, and the occurrence of painful withdrawal symptoms if drinking is ceased. Individuals with an alcohol dependency will begin drinking because it produces a feeling of pleasure or a decrease in anxiety. Eventually, they will require more alcohol to achieve the desired effect. Individuals with a dependency on alcohol who stop drinking often develop severe physical problems including sweating, a rapid pulse, insomnia, nausea, anxiety, or temporary hallucinations. Usually, such an individual continues drinking to avoid these problems and becomes trapped in alcohol dependency.

Alcoholism

The National Council on Alcoholism and Drug Dependence considers alcoholism as a disease that is influenced by social, environmental, and genetic factors. The common features of alcoholism are the inability to control consumption, continued drinking despite negative consequences, and distorted thinking patterns (like irrational denial). It is important to note that alcoholism is not simply the result of a weak will but is a physiological state that requires medical treatment so that it can be controlled. Many individuals may have a problem with alcoholism but not realize it if they are still functioning well overall and only drink in social situations. Alcoholics tend to be those who, even when they aren't drinking, place an undue amount of psychological emphasis on alcohol.

Genetics

Although there is not yet any hard evidence, there is plenty of anecdotal material to suggest that individuals can inherit a predisposition to alcoholism. For instance, the son of an alcoholic white male is four times as likely to develop alcoholism, even if he was adopted by another family at birth. Moreover, the identical twin of an alcoholic is twice as likely as a fraternal twin to develop some disorder related to alcoholism. Brain scans have shown that the sons of alcoholic fathers have a characteristic pattern of brain wave activity. Still, despite this fascinating data, scientists have not yet been able to identify the specific gene or genes that make an individual more susceptible to alcoholism.

Stress and parental alcoholism

It is quite common for an alcoholic to begin drinking to escape psychological problems. Indeed, studies have shown that approximately half the individuals who are diagnosed with alcoholism have another mental disorder. Alcohol is frequently linked with both depression and anxiety disorders. Another common cause of alcoholism is having a parent who abuses alcohol. It has been documented that the children of alcoholics are about five times as likely to develop alcoholism themselves. Perhaps, this is because the children have become accustomed to problems associated with alcoholism, such as poor interpersonal performance, unstable family life, and antisocial tendencies.

<u>Type I and type II classifications</u>

Over the past few decades, the health professionals working towards better prevention and treatment for alcoholism have developed a few different classes of the disease. Type I alcoholics are those who begin a pattern of heavy drinking sometime after the age of 25, often in response to some personal misfortune. These individuals are able to refrain from drinking for a long period of time and feel very conflicted about their drinking problem. Type II alcoholics, on the other hand, usually become dependent on alcohol before the age of 25 and are likely to have a close relative who also has an alcohol problem. These people tend to drink regardless of their personal situation and experience no feelings of guilt or fear regarding their alcoholism.

Adolescent risk behaviors

The Center for Disease Control not only considers alcohol destructive to adolescent health in itself, but believes that it contributes to other behaviors that are damaging to adolescent health. Specifically, the CDC suggests that alcohol contributes to unintentional injuries, fights, academic problems, and illegal behaviors. Over time, alcohol may lead to liver disease, cancer, cardiovascular disease, neurological damage, depression, anxiety, and antisocial tendencies. The rate of alcohol abuse among adolescents has fluctuated a bit in the past years: whereas 50% of high school students admitted to regular drinking in 1999, only 45% said that they were regular drinkers in 2003. Of these, 28% stated that they engaged in regular heavy drinking.

Avoiding alcohol abuse

There are a few guidelines students should know so that they can avoid chronic alcohol abuse. First, never use alcohol as a medicine or as a way to escape personal problems. Always drink slowly, and if possible, alternate alcoholic and nonalcoholic beverages. It is a good idea to eat both before and during drinking, so that less alcohol is rushed into the bloodstream. Drinking should never be the primary reason for a social function, though individuals should try to avoid drinking alone, as well. At a party, it is a good idea to avoid mixed drinks, as it is often difficult to tell just how much alcohol they contain. Finally, and most importantly, every person should have the self-control to say "no" to a drink without feeling guilty or rude.

Tobacco and smoking

Effects of tar and carbon monoxide

When it is burning, tobacco creates tar and carbon monoxide. Tar is a sticky, dark fluid made up of several hundred chemicals. Some of these chemicals are poisonous, and some are carcinogens. When tobacco smoke is inhaled, tar tends to settle in the bronchial tubes of the lungs where it damages the mucus and cilia that are charged with escorting harmful products out of the respiratory system. The smoke from burning tobacco also produces an amount of carbon monoxide about 400 times the amount considered safe by industry. Carbon monoxide is very bad for health: it prevents hemoglobin from carrying oxygen throughout the body, it impairs the nervous system, and is thought to be partly responsible for many heart attacks and strokes.

Tobacco and cancer

The risk of cancer in a smoker rises in proportion to the number of cigarettes smoked daily, the age at which smoking started, and the number of years of smoking. Individuals who smoke two or more packs a day develop lung cancer between 15 and 25 times as often as nonsmokers, though interestingly, precancerous lung tissue will repair itself if the individual quits smoking. Former smokers who have abstained for 15 years develop lung cancer only slightly more often than those who never smoked. The chemicals in cigarette smoke activate an enzyme that in turn produces carcinogens, making the development of cancer more likely among smokers. Smokers with clinical depression are more likely to develop lung cancer, possibly because depression diminishes the effectiveness of the immune system.

Tobacco and respiratory disease

Respiratory function is one of the more immediate processes to be damaged by smoking. Even very new smokers can develop the breathlessness, cough, and excessive phlegm associated with heavy smoking. Smoking is known to contribute to instances of chronic obstructive lung disease, or COLD, a designation which includes both bronchitis and emphysema. These conditions are typically caused by a persistent inability to inhale enough air, which results in the destruction of air sacs and produces a strain on the heart. Chronic bronchitis is the condition in which the production of mucus increases and the bronchial tubes become inflamed, both of which help to narrow the air passages. In short, smoking is the most dangerous form of air pollution.

Stroke risk

Although tobacco use is not usually associated with the risk of stroke, there is clear scientific evidence that links a long-term smoking habit with an increased risk of a debilitating or fatal stroke. Indeed, even when other risk factors are taken into consideration smoking doubles the risk of stroke in men and women. Individuals suffering from hypertension (high blood pressure) exhibit the greatest benefits from quitting. Smoking seems to raise the risk of stroke by weakening the heart muscle, which in turn makes it more difficult for the body to clear blockages in the arteries that can eventually decrease the amount of blood to the brain. Individuals who quit smoking will reduce their risk of stroke, but it will never be quite as low as those who never took up the habit.

Other health problems

There are seemingly countless ways in which smoking can damage health. Smokers are far more likely to develop gum disease or to lose teeth. Even when a smoker practices good oral hygiene, he or she can still suffer from damage to the bones that support teeth. A smoking habit is known to contribute to the formation of mouth and stomach ulcers, and cirrhosis of the liver. Smoking is blamed for a worsening in allergic reactions, diabetes, and hypertension. It is not uncommon for a man who smokes more than ten cigarettes a day to become temporarily impotent. Overall, cigarette smokers tend to miss about one-third more days from work and school than do non-smokers, primarily from respiratory illness. And, of course, there is always the danger of fires that begin when lit cigarettes are left unattended.

Psychological addiction

Tobacco creates in the user certain psychological changes that may become addictive over time. For instance, nicotine is known to stimulate the part of the brain that generates feelings of satisfaction or well-being. Nicotine is also known to temporarily enhance memory, the performance of repetitive tasks, and the tolerance of pain. It is also credited with reducing hunger and anxiety. Individuals suffering from depression may also seek relief through tobacco. Studies have consistently shown that depressed individuals are far more likely than others to develop a smoking habit. Even more troubling, the effects of depression make it much more difficult to quit smoking, so the interdependent relation between tobacco use and depression is likely to continue for a long time.

Physical addiction

Nicotine is consistently shown to be far more addictive than alcohol; whereas only one in ten users of alcohol will eventually become alcoholics, approximately eight of ten heavy smokers will attempt and fail to quit. The method that nicotine uses is similar to that of other addictive substances: it creates an immediate positive feeling when taken; it will cause painful withdrawal symptoms if it is not taken; and it stimulates powerful cravings in the user even after it is removed from the system. Nicotine addiction can become so string that a heavy smoker will experience withdrawal symptoms a mere two hours after smoking. Persistent tobacco use will also lead to an increased tolerance for nicotine, and so the user will have to consume more and more to achieve the pleasure or avoid the pain.

Adolescent risk behaviors

According to the Center for Disease Control, every day about 4000 American teenagers try smoking for the first time. Assuming that conditions remain as they are today, about 6.4 million of today's children will eventually die from a smoking-related illness. The CDC reports that in 2003 22% of high school students smoked cigarettes regularly, and 15% smoked cigars on a regular basis. In addition, about 10% of high school students were users of smokeless tobacco. For the most part, students seem to be more likely to smoke cigarettes if they are from a poor background and if they have parents or friends who are smokers. White males are far more likely to use smokeless tobacco than are any other demographic group.

Advertising, stress, and weight control

Advertising is a culprit in persuading individuals to take up smoking. Critics have pointed out that tobacco advertising targets young people, women, and minorities in ways that are excessive. Because of the harmful effects of tobacco, the government has placed restrictions on tobacco advertising. Many misguided individuals take up smoking to relieve the stress in their lives. Unfortunately, using tobacco as a medication to reduce stress only increases the chance of quickly becoming dependent on it. Some misguided individuals take up smoking because they think it will help them lose weight. Indeed, smokers do tend to burn about 100 more calories every day than non-smokers because of the accelerated metabolism caused by nicotine. Although most people who quit smoking gain a little weight, their increased ability to exercise should enable them to get in shape and be healthier.

Sedative Hypnotics

Sedative hypnotics

Sedative-hypnotics are drugs which depress or slow down the body's functions. Often these drugs are referred to as tranquilizers and sleeping pills or sometimes just as sedatives. Their effects range from calming down anxious people to promoting sleep. Both tranquilizers and sleeping pills can have either effect, depending on how much is taken. At high doses or when they are abused, many of these drugs can even cause unconsciousness and death.

Categories

Barbiturates and benzodiazepines are the two major categories of sedative-hypnotics. The drugs in each of these groups are similar in chemical structure. Some well-known barbiturates are secobarbital (Seconal) and pentobarbital (Nembutal). Diazepam (Valium), chlordiazepoxide (Librium), and clorazepate (Tranxene) are examples of benzodiazepines. A few sedative-hypnotics do not fit in either category. They include methaqualone (Quaalude), ethchlorvynol (Placidyl), chloral hydrate (Noctec), and meprobamate (Miltown). All of these drugs can be dangerous when they are not taken according to a physician's instructions.

Barbiturates

Barbiturates are those drugs that slow down the central nervous system and, in the beginning stages of use, reduce physical and mental tension. Barbiturates are also known to decrease alertness and to induce drowsiness. Besides the obvious risks barbiturates pose to a driver, there is also the danger of slowed breathing, weak heartbeat, disrupted sleep, impaired vision, confusion, chronic lethargy, and irritability. Over a long period of time, many abusers of barbiturates will become dependent on the drug, and may become virtually comatose. Indeed, excessively large doses of barbiturates can immediately result in coma, stupor, or death. There are tremendously painful withdrawal symptoms associated with barbiturates.

Barbiturate use

Barbiturates are often called "barbs" and "downers." Barbiturates that are commonly abused include amobarbital (Amytal), pentobarbital (Nembutal), and secobarbital (Seconal). These drugs are sold in capsules and tablets or sometimes in a liquid form or suppositories. The effects of barbiturates are, in many ways, similar to the effects of alcohol. Small amounts produce calmness and relax muscles. Somewhat larger doses can cause slurred speech, staggering gait, poor judgment, and slow, uncertain reflexes. These effects make it dangerous to drive a car or operate machinery. Large doses can cause unconsciousness and death. Barbiturate overdose is a factor in nearly one-third of all reported drug-related deaths. These include suicides and accidental drug poisonings. Accidental deaths sometimes occur when a user takes one dose, becomes confused and unintentionally takes additional or larger doses. With barbiturates there is less difference between the amount that produces sleep and the amount that kills. Furthermore, barbiturate withdrawal can be more serious than heroin withdrawal.

Therapeutic uses

Barbiturates like pentobarbital and phenobarbital were long used as anxiolytics and hypnotics. Today benzodiazepines have largely supplanted them for these purposes, because benzodiazepines have less potential for abuse and less danger of lethal overdose. Today, fewer than 10 percent of all sedative/hypnotic prescriptions in the United States are for barbiturates. Barbiturates are still widely used in surgical anesthesia, especially to induce anesthesia. Phenobarbital is used as an anticonvulsant for people suffering from seizure disorders such as febrile seizures, tonic-clonic seizures, status epilepticus, and eclampsia.

Depressants

Effects

Depressants slow down the central nervous system. One desired effect is a feeling of relaxation and feeling more at ease in social situations. Another desired effect is a release from inhibitions, enabling us to "let loose" and enjoy ourselves. Slowed down messages from the brain to muscle impair our reflexes, reduce reaction time and impair our coordination, and our ability to drive is impaired.

You would experience this as a slurring of speech, stumbling when you walk, or weaving and a loss of balance. Hand-eye coordination is reduced.

Thought and judgment are impaired because messages between the neurons in the brain are slowed down. Reduced inhibitions and impaired judgment can lead to increased risk for violent behavior.

Examples

Below are examples of depressants:

- Alcohol
- Seconal
- Nembutal
- Amytal
- Tuinal
- Mandrax
- Dalmane
- Halcion
- Valium
- Librium
- Serax

- Ativan
- Xanax
- Inhalants

Narcotics

<u>Effects</u>

Narcotics have the same effects as depressants in that they slow down the central nervous system. They have other effects that depressants do not have, which would include: Pain relief, Suppress cough reaction.

<u>Examples</u>

Below are examples of narcotics:
- Opium
- Codeine
- Morphine
- Heroin
- Methadone
- Demerol
- Dilaudid
- Novahistex-DH
- Novahistine-DH
- Novahistine Expectorant
- Percodan
- Talwin
- Lomotil

Methaqualone

Methaqualone ("Sopors," "ludes") was originally prescribed to reduce anxiety during the day and as a sleeping aid. It is one of the most commonly abused drugs and can cause both physical and psychological dependence. The dangers from abusing methaqualone include injury or death from car accidents caused by faulty judgment and drowsiness, and convulsions, coma, and death from overdose.

Look-alikes

These are pills manufactured to look like real sedative-hypnotics and mimic their effects. Sometimes look-alikes contain over-the-counter drugs such as antihistamines and decongestants, which tend to cause drowsiness. The negative effects can include nausea, stomach cramps, lack of coordination, temporary memory loss, becoming out of touch with the surroundings, and anxious behavior.

Sedatives

A sedative is a substance that depresses the central nervous system (CNS), resulting in calmness, relaxation, reduction of anxiety, sleepiness, and slowed breathing, as well as slurred speech, staggering gait, poor judgment, and slow, uncertain reflexes. Sedatives may be referred to as tranquilizers, depressants, anxiolytics, soporifics, sleeping pills, downers, or sedative-hypnotics. Sedatives can be abused to produce an overly-calming effect (alcohol being the classic and most common sedating drug). At high doses or when they are abused, many of these drugs can cause unconsciousness and even death.

Therapeutic use

Doctors and nurses often administer sedatives to patients in order to dull the patient's anxiety related to painful or anxiety-provoking procedures. Although sedatives do not relieve pain in themselves, they can be a useful adjunct to analgesics in preparing patients for surgery, and are commonly given to patients before they are anaesthetized, or before other highly uncomfortable and invasive procedures like cardiac catheterization, colonoscopy or MRI. They increase tractability and compliance of children or troublesome or demanding patients. Patients in intensive care units are almost always sedated (unless they are unconscious from their condition anyway).

Herbal sedatives, solvent sedatives, nonbenzodiazepine sedatives, and uncategorized sedatives

Herbal sedatives	Solvent sedatives
o catnip	o diethyl ether (Ether)
o mandrake	o gamma-hydroxybutyrate (GHB)
o valerian	Nonbenzodiazepine sedatives
o chloral hydrate (Noctec®)	o zaleplon (Sonata®)
o ethyl alcohol (alcoholic beverage)	o zopiclone (Imovane®, Zimovane®)
o methyl trichloride (Chloroform)	o ethchlorvynol (Placidyl®)
o eszopiclone (Lunesta®)	o ketamine (Ketalar®, Ketaset®)
o zolpidem (Ambien®)	o methyprylon (Noludar®)
Uncategorized sedatives	
o glutethimide (Doriden®)	
o methaqualone (Sopor®, Quaalude®)	
o ramelteon (Rozerem®)	
o Ashwagandha	
o kava (Piper methysticum)	
o marijuana	

Side effects

Activity of the central nervous system becomes slowed down. Small doses relieve tension; large doses produce staggering, blurred vision, impaired perception of time and space, slowed reflexes and breathing, reduced sensitivity to pain, impaired thinking, and slurred speech. Overdoses cause unconsciousness, coma, and death. Accidental overdoses occur when children swallow pills or when adults with increased tolerance are unsure of how many to take.

Combining alcohol and sedative hypnotics

Taken together, alcohol and sedative-hypnotics can kill. The use of barbiturates and other sedative-hypnotics with other drugs that slow down the body, such as alcohol, multiplies their effects and greatly increases the risk of death. Overdose deaths can occur when barbiturates and alcohol are used together, either deliberately or accidentally.

Abuse and overdose

Sedative-hypnotics can be abused, including the benzodiazepines. Diazepam (Valium), chlordiazepoxide (Librium), and chlorazepate (Tranxene) are examples of benzodiazepines. These drugs are also sold on the street as downers. As with the barbiturates, tolerance and dependence can develop if benzodiazepines are taken regularly in high doses over prolonged periods of time. Other sedative-hypnotics which are abused include glutethimide (Doriden), ethchlorvynol (Placidyl), and methaqualone (Sopor, Quaalude).

All sedatives can be abused, but barbiturates and benzodiazepines are responsible for most of the problems with sedative abuse due to their widespread "recreational" or non-medical use. People who have difficulty dealing with stress, anxiety or sleeplessness may overuse or become dependent on sedatives. Heroin users take them either to supplement their drug or to substitute for it. Stimulant users frequently take sedatives to calm excessive jitteriness. Others take sedatives recreationally to relax and forget their worries. Barbiturate overdose is a factor in nearly one-third of all reported drug-related deaths. These include suicides and accidental drug poisonings. Accidental deaths sometimes occur when a drowsy, confused user repeats doses, or when sedatives are taken with alcohol. In the U.S., in 1998, a total of 70,982 sedative exposures were reported to U.S. poison control centers, of which 2310 (3.2%) resulted in major toxicity and 89 (0.1%) resulted in death. About half of all the people admitted to emergency rooms in the U.S. as a result of nonmedical use of sedatives have a legitimate prescription for the drug, but have taken an excessive dose or combined it with alcohol or other drugs.

Antidepressants, barbiturates, and Benzodiazepines

Antidepressants
- mirtazapine (Remeron®)
- trazodone (Desyrel®)

Barbiturates
- amobarbital (Amytal®)
- pentobarbital (Nembutal®)
- secobarbital (Seconal®)

Benzodiazepines ("minor tranquilizers")
- alprazolam (Xanax®)
- bromazepam (Lexotan®)
- clonazepam (Klonopin®)
- diazepam (Valium®)
- estazolam (Prosom®)
- flunitrazepam (Rohypnol®)
- lorazepam (Ativan®)

- midazolam (Versed®)
- nitrazepam (Mogadon®)
- oxazepam (Serax®)
- triazolam (Halcion®)
- temazepam (Restoril®, Normison®, Planum®, Tenox® and Temaze®)
- chlordiazepoxide (Librium®)

Typical antipsychotics, atypical antipsychotics, and sedating antihistamines

Typical antipsychotics ("major tranquilizers")
- chlorpromazine (Thorazine®, Largactil®)
- fluphenazine (Prolixin®)
- haloperidol (Haldol®)
- loxapine succinate (Loxitane®)
- perphenazine (Etrafon®, Trilafon®)
- prochlorperazine (Compazine®)
- thiothixene (Navane®)
- trifluoperazine (Stelazine®, Trifluoperaz®)
- zuclopentixol (Cisordinol®)

Atypical antipsychotics
- clozapine (Clozaril®)
- olanzapine (Zyprexa®)
- quetiapine (Seroquel®)
- risperidone (Risperdal®)
- ziprasidone (Geodon®) (May cause somnolence in some, while causing insomnia in others)

Sedating antihistamines

- clemastine

- doxylamine

- diphenhydramine (Benadryl®)

- hydroxyzine (Atarax®)

- niaprazine

- promethazine

- pyribenzamine

Hypnotics

Hypnotic drugs induce sleep (which differentiates them from the sedative category), used in the treatment of insomnia and in surgical anesthesia. Often the treatment of insomnia will not begin with drugs at all. Since many hypnotic drugs are habit-forming, a physician will usually recommend alternative sleeping patterns and exercise before prescribing medication for sleep, due to a large number of factors known to disturb the human sleep pattern.

These drugs include barbiturates, opioids, benzodiazepines (not all, hypnotic benzodiazepines are usually more powerful than the others in their group), zolpidem, zaleplon, zopiclone, eszopiclone, chloral hydrate, Levomepromazine, chlormethiazole or the antihistamines doxylamine, promethazine, and diphenhydramine. Alcohol is also used as a hypnotic drug.

Hypnotic barbiturate use and dependence

Barbiturate use can lead to both psychological and physical dependence. Psychological addiction can occur quickly. Signs of drug dependence include relying on a drug regularly for a desired effect. The addicted abuser believes he must take a barbiturate to sleep, relax, or just get through the day. Continued use of barbiturates leads to physical dependence. As people develop a tolerance for barbiturates, they may need more of the drug or a higher dosage to get the desired effect. This can lead to an overdose, which results when a person takes a larger-than-prescribed dose of a drug. People who get in the habit of taking sleeping pills every night to fall asleep may start out with one per night, progress to two, and then graduate to four to get the same effect. Eventually the dose they need to fall asleep may also be that which stops their breathing. Generally, barbiturate overdoses occur because due to tolerance, the effective dose approaches the lethal dose. Symptoms of an overdose typically include severe weakness, confusion, shortness of breath, extreme drowsiness, an unusually slow heartbeat, and darting eye movements. The amount of a fatal dosage of barbiturate varies from one individual to another, but the lethal dose is usually 10 to 15 times as large as a usual dose. An overdose affects the heart and the respiratory system and the user falls into a coma and dies. Barbiturates can have a 'multiplying' effect when taken with other depressants, such as alcohol. Combining barbiturates and alcohol can increase the effects by as much as ten times, resulting in death.

Hypnotic barbiturates and alcohol

Recreational users report that a barbiturate high makes them feel "relaxed, sociable, and good-humored". Users typically describe feelings of decreased anxiety, a loss of inhibitions, and an increased sense of confidence. Physical effects include slowed breathing and a lowering of both blood pressure and heart rate. Like alcohol, barbiturates are intoxicating. During the stage after mild intoxication, the user's speech may be slurred and a loss of coordination may become noticeable. Stumbling and staggering are common. Other symptoms include shallow breathing, fatigue, frequent yawning, and irritability. When taken in high doses, barbiturates can cause serious side effects, including "unpredictable emotional reactions and mental confusion". Judgment becomes severely impaired and the user may experience mood swings. The mental effects of barbiturates generally depend on the amount of the drug taken and the strength of the dosage. Generally, a person falls asleep when taking a prescribed dosage at bedtime. But barbiturates remain in the system for a long time. At normal doses the major concern is that they can have sedative effects that outlast their sleep-inducing properties. Driving, flying an airplane, or other activities requiring muscle coordination can be impaired for up to a day after a single dose. Some barbiturates can be detected in a user's urine sample days or even weeks after the drug was consumed.

Dependence

They can cause both physical and psychological dependence. Regular use over a long period of time may result in tolerance, which means people have to take larger and larger doses to get the same effects. When regular users stop using large doses of these drugs suddenly, they may develop physical withdrawal symptoms ranging from restlessness, insomnia and anxiety, to convulsions and death. When users become psychologically dependent, they feel as if they need the drug to function. Finding and using the drug becomes the main focus in life.

Symptoms of dependence include tolerance resulting in higher levels needed to achieve the same calming effect. Symptoms of psychological dependence include needing the drug to function and being obsessed with obtaining the drug. Symptoms of withdrawal are restlessness, insomnia, anxiety, seizures, and even death in some cases.

To be clinically diagnosed as dependent on a substance, 3 or more of the following symptoms must be exhibited simultaneously during a 12-month period:

- Amount and duration of substance intake is longer than intended
- Efforts to control intake are not successful
- A great deal of effort is put into obtaining, using, or recovering from effects of the substance
- Due to use of substance, other activities (social, work-related, leisure) are reduced or abandoned
- Substance is used even when known to cause or exacerbate a persistent or recurrent psychological, or physical problem
- Tolerance of the substance
- Withdrawal from the substance

Stimulants

Stimulants

Stimulant drugs are drugs that temporarily increase alertness and awareness. They usually have increased side-effects with increased effectiveness, and the more ·powerful variants are therefore often prescription medicines or illegal drugs. Stimulants increase the activity of either the sympathetic nervous system, the central nervous system (CNS) or both. Some stimulants produce a sense of euphoria, in particular the stimulants which exert influence on the CNS. Stimulants are used therapeutically to increase or maintain alertness, to counteract fatigue in situations where sleep is not practical (e.g. while operating vehicles), to counteract abnormal states that diminish alertness consciousness (such as in narcolepsy), to promote weight loss (phentermine) as well as to enhance the ability to concentrate in people diagnosed with attentional disruptions (especially ADHD). Occasionally, they are also used to treat depression. Stimulants are sometimes used to boost endurance and productivity as well as to suppress appetite, and therefore are also known to promote eating disorders such as anorexia if abused. The euphoria produced by some stimulants leads to their recreational use, although this is illegal in most jurisdictions. Caffeine, found in beverages such as coffee and soft drinks, as well as nicotine, which is found in tobacco, are among some of the world's most commonly used stimulants. Examples of other well known stimulants include ephedrine, amphetamines, cocaine, methylphenidate, MDMA, and modafinil. Stimulants are commonly referred to in slang as "uppers". Stimulants with significant abuse potential are very carefully controlled substances in America and may either be legally available only by prescription (e.g., methamphetamine as Desoxyn), or not at all (e.g. methcathinone).

Effects

Stimulants speed up the central nervous system. Desired effects would include a sense of well being or euphoria, or an enhanced ability to think and function. Other effects include anxiety, paranoia, increased heart rate, increased blood pressure, reduced appetite, restlessness, insomnia, and a feeling of being "shaky."

Examples

Some examples of stimulants are:

- Cocaine
- Dexedrine
- Methedrine
- Tenuate
- Ionamin
- Ritalin
- Fastin
- Tobacco
- Caffeine

Amphetamines

An amphetamine is one of a class of sympathomimetic amines with powerful stimulant action on the central nervous system. This class includes amphetamine, dexamphetamine, and methamphetamine. Often referred to as "speed," sympathomimetics exhibit symptoms and signs including tachycardia, pupillary dilatation, elevated blood pressure, hyperreflexia, sweating, chills, anorexia, nausea or vomiting, insomnia, and abnormal behavior such as aggression, grandiosity, hyper vigilance, agitation, and impaired judgment. In rare cases, delirium develops within 24 hours of use. Chronic use commonly induces personality and behavior changes such as impulsivity, aggressivity, irritability, suspiciousness, and paranoid psychosis. Cessation of intake after prolonged or heavy use may produce a withdrawal reaction, with depressed mood, fatigue, hyperphagia, sleep disturbance, and increased dreaming. Currently, prescription of amphetamines and related substances is limited principally to the treatment of narcolepsy and ADHD. Use of these agents as anorectic agents in the treatment of obesity is discouraged.

For a long time, amphetamines were prescribed to control weight gain. Now, however, doctors have decided that these powerful stimulants can be extremely addictive and dangerous to health. Some common names of amphetamines are Benzedrine, Dexedrine, and Methedrine. Other substances that are related to amphetamines include Ritalin, Cylert, and Preludin. Amphetamines are usually taken orally, though they may also be snorted, smoked, or injected. Some forms of methamphetamine are extremely addictive and can have effects lasting from between twelve to fourteen hours. These products all trigger the release of adrenaline, which stimulates the central nervous system and raises the heart rate.

Amphetamines increase the heart and respiration rates, increase blood pressure and in some users, dilate the pupils of the eyes and decrease appetite. Like NDRIs, amphetamine increases the levels of norepinephrine and dopamine in the brain via reuptake inhibition; however, the more important mechanism by which amphetamines cause stimulation is through the direct release of these catecholamines from storage vesicles in cells. Amphetamines are known to cause elevated mood and euphoria as well as rebound depression and anxiety. Other possible effects include blurred vision, insomnia, and dizziness.

Amphetamines are sometimes prescribed therapeutically by physicians and their availability makes them prime candidates for misuse. Used properly, amphetamines increase alertness, concentration and physical endurance. They are often prescribed to counter the effects of narcolepsy, a disorder marked by episodes of uncontrollable sleep, and to help patients with learning disabilities such as ADD and ADHD. On occasion, major depression is treated with amphetamines as well.

Amphetamines can be used as an add-on to antidepressant therapy as well, with some success in certain populations.

Amphetamine psychosis

Amphetamine psychosis is a disorder characterized by paranoid delusions, frequently accompanied by auditory or tactile hallucinations, hyperactivity, and lability of mood, which develops during or shortly after repeated use of moderate or high doses of amphetamines. Typically, the individual's behavior is hostile and irrational, and may result in unprovoked violence. In most cases there is no clouding of consciousness, but an acute delirium is occasionally seen after the ingestion of very high doses. The disorder is included in category psychotic disorder, alcohol- or drug-induced.

Effects and risks

Amphetamines make the user very alert and full of energy. Users typically report a feeling of well-being and confidence, and a sense that they are thinking very clearly, even though research does not indicate that this is so. Amphetamine users are very talkative and animated, to the point of being uncomfortably restless. Large dosages will produce confusion, incoherent speech, anxiety, and even heart palpitations. In the short-term, amphetamine use can cause heart trouble, a loss of coordination, anger, nausea, or chills. Over the long term, it may cause malnutrition, skin disorders, insomnia, depression, vitamin deficiencies, and brain damage affecting the areas controlling speech. Withdrawing from amphetamines can also be a very difficult and painful process.

Famous methamphetamine users

Some famous adults who have used methamphetamines are President John F. Kennedy and Adolf Hitler. John F. Kennedy would take a shot to help him cope with his chronic back pain. Adolf Hitler use to receive up to eight injections of meth every day. It was also found that during World War II soldiers were given methamphetamines in order to fight hunger and fatigue.

Phenethylamines

Phenethylamine is an alkaloid and monoamine and believed to be a neuromodulator or neurotransmitter. Furthermore it is the basic chemical structure behind most stimulants, especially sympathomimetic amines. Common phenethylamines include:

- catecholamines: dopamine, epinephrine, and norepinephrine
- plant alkaloids: ephedrine, pseudoephedrine, cathinone, cathine
- amphetamines and substituted amphetamines: amphetamine, methamphetamine, MDA, MDMA, MDMC, DOM, DOB, DOI
- methylphenidate
- bronchodilators: albuterol, clenbuterol
- psychedelics: 2C (psychedelics), mescaline

MDMA

Methylenedioxymethamphetamine (MDMA) is a drug that comes either in tablet or capsule form (known as ecstasy, zoom, scrap), as a powder or crystal. Stimulant effects of MDMA include increased blood pressure and heart rate, loss of appetite, rapid sweating, and a dry mouth and throat. Ecstasy pills often contain amounts of other drugs which may include any of a wide range of substances such as MDA, MDEA, MBDB, PCP, DXM, Ketamine, Caffeine, Amphetamine, Methamphetamine, Ephedrine, Pseudoephedrine, Aspirin, Paracetamol, and, in a small number of cases, PMA, Cocaine, Fentanyl, mCPP, BZP+TFMPP, DOB, and 2C-B. In some cases the substance sold as ecstasy may not contain MDMA at all.

MDMA has emerged as one of the most common and dangerous drugs of the past decade. Originally developed as a solution to social anxiety and depression, Ecstasy has become popular as a recreational drug among young people. Although users of the drug report that it causes a feeling of happiness and euphoria, they, also report some troubling side effects. Ecstasy has been linked with insomnia, nausea, fatigue, and problems in concentrating. It is particularly dangerous to take the drug in a chaotic and hot environment, like a dance club, because it causes dehydration to a dangerous degree. There have been scores of deaths blamed on Ecstasy; most of the time, this was because the user raised their body temperature to around 110° Fahrenheit. MDMA was historically used in a therapeutic setting by a small number of psychiatrists for marriage counseling, before it was outlawed by the DEA because of its widespread recreational use. As of 2001, it is being considered by the FDA in the treatment of Post-traumatic stress disorder. It is also being evaluated for possible usages in palliative care.

Cocaine

Cocaine is made from the leaves of the coca shrub, which grows in the mountain regions of South American countries such as Bolivia, Colombia, and Peru. In Europe and North America, the most common form of cocaine is a white crystalline powder. Cocaine is a stimulant but is not normally prescribed therapeutically for its stimulant properties, although it sees clinical use as a local anesthetic, particularly in ophthalmology. Most cocaine use is recreational and its abuse potential is high, and so its sale and possession are strictly controlled in most jurisdictions. Other tropane derivative drugs related to cocaine are also known such as troparil and lometopane but have not been widely sold or used recreationally.

Cocaine and its deadly derivative, crack, are among the most addictive and deadly substances that are commonly abused. When they are taken, whether through inhalation or intravenous injection, they accelerate the mental and physical processes and create in the mind of the user a feeling of invulnerability and high energy. They may cause health problems in the short term, ranging from headaches and shaking to seizures, collapse, and death. Over the long term, cocaine and crack users usually have impaired sexual function, blood pressure problems, heart trouble, brain hemorrhaging, hepatitis, and malnutrition. Users of these drugs are also more likely to contract the HIV virus. Cocaine users frequently become paranoid, angry, and suspicious.

NDRIs

Norepinephrine and Dopamine Reuptake Inhibitors (NDRIs)

These compounds inhibit the uptake of the monoamines dopamine and norepinephrine into storage vesicles, effectively increasing their amounts in the brain and causing a stimulating effect. Many of these compounds are effective ADHD medications and antidepressants. The most popular and well-known dopamine and norepinephrine reuptake inhibitor antidepressant is bupropion (Wellbutrin). Other examples of NDRIs include MDPV, pyrovalerone, mazindol and pipradrol. Although these medicines have similar methods of action to stimulants, they are less popular for abuse (thus not scheduled) and have an extended release mechanism or a very long half life. Many NDRIs are also phenethylamines.

Nicotine

Nicotine is an alkaloid found in the nightshade family of plants (Solanaceae), predominantly in tobacco, and in lower quantities in tomato, potato, eggplant (aubergine), and green pepper. Nicotine alkaloids are also found in the leaves of the coca plant. Nicotine constitutes 0.3 to 5% of the tobacco plant by dry weight, with biosynthesis taking place in the roots, and accumulates in the leaves. It is a potent nerve poison and is included in many insecticides. The primary therapeutic use of nicotine is in treating nicotine dependence in order to eliminate smoking with its risks to health. In very low concentrations, nicotine acts as a stimulant, and it is one of the main factors responsible for the dependence-forming properties of tobacco smoking. Although pure nicotine is noncarcinogenic, its presence may inhibit the body's ability to cull aberrant cells.

Caffeine

Caffeine is a drug that is found naturally in coffee, tea, and to a small extent cocoa. It is also found in many soft drinks, particularly energy drinks like Mountain Dew and Monster. Caffeine stimulates the body, increasing heart rate and blood pressure, and alertness, making some people feel better and able to concentrate. Caffeine is also a diuretic. The vast majority (over 80%) of people in the United States consume caffeine on a daily basis. As a result, few jurisdictions restrict its sale and use. Caffeine is also sold in some countries as an isolated drug (as opposed to its natural occurrence in many foods). It serves as a mild stimulant to ward off sleepiness and sees wide use among people who must remain alert in their work (e.g., truck drivers, military members). Some medications contain caffeine as one of their minor active ingredients, often for the purpose of enhancing the effect of the main ingredient or reducing one of its side effects.

Ampakines

Recently, there have been improvements in the area of stimulant pharmacology, producing a class of chemicals known as Ampakines, or eugeroics, (good arousal). These stimulants tend to increase alertness without the peripheral (body) effects or addiction/tolerance/abuse potential of the traditional stimulants. They have minimal effect on sleep structure, and do not cause rebound hypersomnolence or "come down" effects. Currently, there are two stimulants in this class being used: modafinil and adrafinil, marketed as Provigil and Olmifon, respectively. Newer ampakines such as ampalex and CX717 have been developed but are still in clinical trials and have not yet been sold commercially. Another compound with similar effects to these drugs is Carphedon, which is sold as a general stimulant in Russia under the brand name Phenotropil.

Methylphenidate for ADHD

Attention deficit/ hyperactivity disorder is the diagnosis given to a range of conditions in which the individual has a hard time controlling motion or sustaining attention. Although ADHD is typically thought of as a disorder that affects children, new research suggests that it is not outgrown, and that adults may be just as likely to suffer from it. Individuals suffering from ADHD are impulsive, constantly in motion, and easily distracted. They may feel perpetually restless, may be unusually forgetful, and are likely to be socially immature. Most of those who suffer from ADHD are benefited by behavioral therapy and medication. Methylphenidate is a medication prescribed for individuals (usually children) who have attention-deficit hyperactivity disorder (ADHD), which consists of a persistent pattern of abnormally high levels of activity, impulsivity, and/or inattention that is more frequently displayed and more severe than is typically observed in individuals with comparable levels of development.

Diet products

Everyone has seen the advertisements for diet pills that promise to reduce weight with minimal effort. As recently as the 1970's, American women were sold so-called diet pills that were nothing but amphetamines. Even today, the diet pill and weight-loss product industry is enormous. However, many of these products pose a risk to health. In addition, diet pills may not even effectively reduce weight because the individuals who take them may feel empowered to eat as much as they like. Liquid diets should also be avoided in most cases. Although today's liquid diets offer a more comprehensive range of proteins, carbohydrates, vitamins, and minerals than those of the past, anyone considering their use should still seek medical advice.

Opioids

Opioids

The opioid family of narcotics relaxes the central nervous system and provides a temporary relief to physical pain. They also produce a short-term sense of mental well-being and satisfaction. They have serious health consequences, however. Opioids are blamed for restlessness, nausea, weight loss, loss of sex drive, slurred speech, sweating, drowsiness, and impaired judgment, attention, and memory. Over time, many individuals will become extremely addicted to opioids and will suffer from malnutrition, an impaired immune system, infections of the heart and lungs, hepatitis, tetanus, depression, skin abscesses, and even the HIV virus. It is also possible to overdose on opioids and lapse into a coma or die.

Opiates and morphinomometics

Morphine, the archetypal opioid, and various other substances (e.g. codeine, oxycodone, hydrocodone, diamorphine, pethidine) all exert a similar influence on the cerebral opioid receptor system. Tramadol and buprenorphine are thought to be partial agonists of the opioid receptors. Dosing of all opioids may be limited by opioid toxicity (confusion, respiratory depression, myoclonic jerks and pinpoint pupils), but there is no dose ceiling in patients who tolerate this.

Opioids, while very effective analgesics, may have some unpleasant side-effects. Up to 1 in 3 patients starting morphine may experience nausea and vomiting. Pruritus (itching) may require switching to a different opioid. Constipation occurs in almost all patients on opioids, and laxatives are typically co-prescribed.

When used appropriately, opioids and similar narcotic analgesics are otherwise safe and effective; however risks such as addiction and the body becoming used to the drug can occur. Due to the body getting used to the drug often the dose must be increased if it is for a chronic disease this is where the no ceiling limit of the drug comes into play. However what must be remembered is although there is no upper limit there is a still a toxic dose even if the body has become used to lower doses.

Narcotics

The term "narcotic," derived from the Greek word for stupor, originally referred to a variety of substances that dulled the senses and relieved pain. Today, the term is used in a number of ways. Some individuals define narcotics as those substances that bind at opioid receptors (cellular membrane proteins activated by substances like heroin or morphine) while others refer to any illicit substance as a narcotic. In a legal context, narcotic refers to opium, opium derivatives, and their semi-synthetic substitutes. Cocaine and coca leaves, which are also classified as "narcotics" in the Controlled Substances Act (CSA), neither bind opioid receptors nor produce morphine-like effects, and are considered stimulants. For the purposes of this discussion, the term narcotic refers to drugs that produce morphine-like effects. Narcotics are used therapeutically to treat pain, suppress cough, alleviate diarrhea, and induce anesthesia. Narcotics are administered in a variety of ways. Some are taken orally, transdermally (skin patches), or injected. They are also available in suppositories. As drugs of abuse, they are often smoked, sniffed, or injected. Drug effects depend heavily on the dose, route of administration, and previous exposure to the drug. Aside from their medical use, narcotics produce a general sense of well-being by reducing tension, anxiety and aggression. These effects are helpful in a therapeutic setting but contribute to their abuse.

PCA

Patient-controlled analgesia (PCA) is any method of allowing a person in pain to administer their own pain relief. The most common form of this is the paracetamol that many keep in their bathroom cabinet. If a complaint, for example a headache, does not resolve with a small dose of painkiller, more may be taken up to a maximum dose. This situation has the patient in control, and is in fact the most common patient-controlled analgesia. As pain is a combination of tissue damage and emotional state, being in control means reducing the emotional component of pain. PCA has passed into medical jargon to mean the electronically controlled infusion pump that delivers a prescribed amount of intravenous or epidural analgesic to the patient when he or she activates a button. Opioids are the medication most often administered through PCAs. PCA was introduced by Dr. Philip H. Sechzer in the later 1960s and described in 1971.

Among the benefits of this device are:
- It saves time between when the patient feels pain and/or the need to receive analgesia and when it is administered (activation automatically pumps the dose into a pre- existing IV line into the patient).
- It reduces workload of the nursing staff (an amount of the prescribed analgesic is pre-loaded into the PCA, enough for multiple doses).
- It reduces the chances for medication errors (the PCA is programmed per the physician's order for amount and interval between doses and "locks out" the patient if he or she attempts to self- administer too often.)
- Patients can receive medicine when they need it, instead of having to wait for nursing staff, and tend to use less.
- Patients who use PCAs report better analgesia and lower pain scores than those patients who have to request analgesia from the nursing staff when they are in pain.

- PCA provides a measurement of how much pain an individual patient is experiencing from one day to the next.
- It involves patients in their own care, giving them control and ultimately rendering better patient outcomes.

Disadvantages are:

- Patients may be unwilling to use the PCA or be physically or mentally unable to. (In a lot of cases physical inability can be mitigated through use of an eye gaze, sip-puff or alternative switch access method). PCA pumps are rated among the worlds most accessible pieces of equipment since all manufacturers must have alternative switch access built into their PCA pumps. Most companies will use a TASH approved switch interface connection as TASH is one of the industry standards in accessibility switches.
- The pumps are often expensive and may malfunction. (Malfunctions are usually limited, and many malfunctions result from an improperly maintained/charged battery.)
- More importantly, the dosing regimen may be set so that the patient does not receive enough analgesia (bolus doses set too small, lock-out too long). When the patient sleeps, the analgesic wears off so they wake in pain. This is sometimes countered by setting a background continuous infusion of the analgesia.

Narcotic analgesic addiction

In the United States in recent years, there has been a wave of new addictions to prescription narcotics such as oxycodone (such as OxyContin, or with acetaminophen, as Percocet) and hydrocodone (commonly prescribed with acetaminophen, as in Vicodin, Lortab etc.) when available in pure formulations as opposed to combined with other medications (as in Percocet which contains both oxycodone and acetaminophen/paracetamol). Hydrocodone is only available in pure form in some European countries as the original hydrocodone pharmaceutical, Dicodid tablets. Far from reducing addiction liability, the paracetamol content of many codeine, dihydrocodeine, hydrocodone, and oxycodone pharmaceuticals in the United States only saddles users with the high risk of severe liver damage, and extraction of the opioids with cold water or solvents reduces this problem for the sophisticated abuser, self-medicator, and legitimate prescription holder alike.

Hallucinogens

Hallucinogens

Hallucinogens are substances such as LSD, mescaline, and psilocybin that create profound changes in the mind's ability to function. When taken, hallucinogens produce visions and temporary feelings of satisfaction and euphoria. They may also lead to increases in heart rate, blood pressure, and body temperature. Hallucinogens are associated with headaches, nausea, sweating, trembling, heart palpitations, and poor coordination. More serious, perhaps, is the possibility of having an extremely traumatic psychological experience while under the influence of one of these drugs. Many individuals report long-term, possibly permanent side effects from hallucinogens. These side effects may include depression, flashbacks, and delusions.

Examples

Examples of hallucinogens are:
- LSD
- PCP
- MDA
- Mescaline or Peyote

- DMT
- Psilocybin
- STP or DOM
- PMA
- Cannabis

Categories

The general group of pharmacological agents commonly known as hallucinogens can be divided into three broad categories: psychedelics, dissociatives, and deliriants. These classes of psychoactive drugs have in common that they can cause subjective changes in perception, thought, emotion and consciousness. Unlike other psychoactive drugs, such as stimulants and opioids, the hallucinogens do not merely amplify familiar states of mind, but rather induce experiences that are qualitatively different from those of ordinary consciousness. These experiences are often compared to non-ordinary forms of consciousness such as trance, meditation, conversion experiences, and dreams.

Psychedelics, dissociatives, and deliriants

Psychedelics, dissociatives, and deliriants have a long history of use within medicinal and religious traditions around the world. They are used in shamanic forms of ritual healing and divination, in initiation rites, and in religious rituals. When used in religious practice, psychedelic drugs, as well as other substances like tobacco, are referred to as entheogens.

LSD

Dr. Albert Hofmann, whose discovery of LSD led to wide-spread Western interest in psychedelics starting in the mid-20th century, psychedelic drugs have been the object of extensive attention in the Western world. They have been and are being explored as potential therapeutic agents in treating depression, Post-traumatic Stress Disorder, Obsessive-compulsive Disorder, alcoholism, opioid addiction, cluster headaches, and other ailments. Early military research focused on their use as incapacitating agents. Intelligence agencies tested these drugs in the hope that they would provide an effective means of interrogation, with little success.

Psychedelics

The word psychedelic was coined to express the idea of a drug that makes manifest a hidden but real aspect of the mind. It is commonly applied to any drug with perception-altering effects such as LSD, psilocybin, DMT, 2C-B, mescaline, and DOM as well as a panoply of other tryptamines, phenethylamines and yet more exotic chemicals, all of which appear to act mainly on the 5-HT2A receptor. Common herbal sources of psychedelics include psilocybe mushrooms, various ayahuasca preparations, peyote, San Pedro cactus, and the seeds of morning glory and Hawaiian baby woodrose.

Psychedelic effects can vary depending on the precise drug, dosage, set, and setting. "Trips" range between the short but intense effects of intravenous DMT to the protracted ibogaine experience, which can last for days. Appropriate dosage ranges from extremely low (LSD) to rather high (mescaline). Some drugs, like the auditory hallucinogen DIPT, act specifically to distort a single sense, and others have more diffuse effects on cognition generally. Some are more conducive to solitary experiences, while others are positively empathogenic. Many psychedelics (LSD, psilocybin, mescaline and numerous others) are non-toxic, making it difficult to overdose on these compounds.

One thing that most of these drugs do not do, despite the ingrained usage of the term hallucinogen, is to cause hallucination. Hallucinations, strictly speaking, are perceptions that have no basis in reality, but that appear entirely realistic. A typical "hallucination" induced by a psychedelic drug is more accurately described as a modification of regular perception, and the subject is usually quite aware of the illusory and personal nature of their perceptions. Some less common drugs, such as dimethyltryptamine and atropine, may cause hallucinations in the proper sense. Yet the most popular, and at the same time most stigmatized, use of psychedelics in Western culture has been associated with the search for direct religious experience, enhanced creativity, personal development, and "mind expansion". The use of psychedelic drugs was a major element of the 1960s counterculture, where it became associated with various political movements and a general atmosphere of rebellion and strife between generations. Despite prohibition, the recreational, spiritual, and medical use of psychedelics continues today.

Nature, cause, and description of effects: Much debate exists not only about the nature and causes, but even about the very description of the effects of psychedelic drugs. One prominent tradition involves the "reducing valve" concept, first articulated in Aldous Huxley's book The Doors of Perception. In this view, the drugs disable the brain's "filtering" ability to selectively prevent certain perceptions, emotions, memories and thoughts from ever reaching the conscious mind. This effect has been described as mind expanding, or consciousness expanding, for the drug "expands" the realm of experience available to conscious awareness. A large number of drugs, such as cannabis and Ecstasy, produce effects that could be classified as psychedelic (especially at higher doses) but are not considered to be strictly psychedelic drugs due to other effects that may be more (or equally) prevalent, such as sedation or disinhibition. In addition, drugs such as cannabis do not affect serotonin receptors like "true" psychedelics.

Long term use: Most psychedelics are not known to have long-term physical toxicity. However, amphetamine-like psychedelics, such as MDMA, that release neurotransmitters may stimulate increased formation of free radicals possibly formed from neurotransmitters released from the synaptic vesicle. Free radicals are associated with cell damage in other contexts, and have been suggested to be involved in many types of mental conditions including Parkinson's disease, senility, schizophrenia, and Alzheimer's. The same concerns do not apply to psychedelics that do not release neurotransmitters, such as LSD, nor to dissociatives and deliriants. No clear connection has been made between psychedelic drugs and organic brain damage; however, high doses over time of some dissociatives and deliriants have been shown to cause Olney's lesions in other animals, and have been suspected to occur in humans. Additionally, hallucinogen persisting perception disorder (HPPD) is a diagnosed condition where some effects of drugs persist after a long time--although medical technology has yet to determine what causes the condition.

Dissociatives

Dissociatives are drugs that reduce (or block) signals to the conscious mind from other parts of the brain, typically the physical senses. Such a state of sensory deprivation can facilitate self exploration, hallucinations, and dreamlike states of mind which may resemble some psychedelic mindstates. Essentially similar states of mind can be reached via contrasting paths—psychedelic or dissociative. That said, the entire experience, risks and benefits are markedly different.

The primary dissociatives are similar in action to PCP (angel dust) and include ketamine (an anesthetic), and dextromethorphan (an active ingredient in many cough syrups). Also included are nitrous oxide, and muscimol from the Amanita muscaria mushroom.

Many dissociatives also have CNS depressant effects, thereby carrying similar risks as opioids to slowing breathing or heart rate to levels resulting in death (when using very high doses). This does not appear to be true in other cases; and the principal risk of nitrous oxide seems to be due to oxygen deprivation. Injury from falling is also a danger, as nitrous oxide may cause sudden loss of consciousness, an effect of oxygen deprivation.

Deliriants

Deliriants are sometimes called true hallucinogens, because they do cause hallucinations in the proper sense: a user may have conversations with people who aren't there, or become angry at a 'person' mimicking their actions, not realizing it is their own reflection in a mirror. They are called deliriants because their effects are similar to the experiences of people with delirious fevers. While dissociatives can produce effects similar to lucid dreaming (where one is consciously aware they are dreaming), the deliriants have effects akin to sleepwalking (where one doesn't remember what happened during the experience).

The deliriants are a special class of dissociative which are antagonists for the acetylcholine receptors. Included in this group are such plants as deadly nightshade, mandrake, henbane and datura, as well as a number of pharmaceutical drugs when taken in very high doses such as the first generation antihistamines diphenhydramine (Benadryl), its close relative dimenhydrinate (Dramamine or Gravol), and hydroxyzine, to name a few. In addition to the danger of being far more "out of it" than with other drugs, and retaining a truly fragmented dissociation from regular consciousness without being immobilized, the anticholinergics are toxic, can cause death due to overdose, and also include a number of uncomfortable side effects. These side effects include dehydration and mydriasis (dilation of the pupils). Most modern-day "psychonauts" who use deliriants report similar or identical hallucinations and challenges. Diphenhydramine, as well as Dimenhydrinate, when taken in a high enough dose, evokes vivid, dark, and entity-like hallucinations, peripheral disturbances, feelings of being alone but simultaneously of being watched, and hallucinations of real things ceasing to exist. Deliriants also may cause confusion or even rage, and thus have been used by ancient peoples as a battle stimulant

PCP

Phencyclidine, otherwise known as PCP or angel dust, is one of the more dangerous drugs that are commonly abused. When it is taken, it immediately produces a profound change in perceptions, including hallucinations and delusions of personal strength. Individuals on PCP may incorrectly believe that they are invulnerable. Besides the obvious risks associated with this psychological condition, PCP users will experience flushing, an increase in heart rate, diminished sensitivity to pain, impaired coordination and speech, and possibly be put into a stupor. The use of PCP can cause a psychosis, will increase the risk of danger to the user and those around the user, and can cause immediate coma and death.

Pharmacological classes of hallucinogens

One possible way of classifying the hallucinogens is by their chemical structure and that of the receptors they act on. In this vein, the following categories are often used:

- Psychedelics (serotonin 5-HT2A receptor agonists)
- Tryptamines
  - Lysergamides
- Phenethylamines
  - Substituted phenethylamines
  - Substituted amphetamines
  - Empathogens and/or Entactogens (serotonin releasers)
- Cannabinoids (CB-1 cannabinoid receptor agonists)
- Dissociatives
  - NMDA receptor antagonists and sigma1 ligands
  - Inhalants
  - Cholinergics
- Deliriants (anticholinergics)
  - Tropanes

- Antihistamines

History of hallucinogens

Before and during World War II

Hallucinogenic drugs are among the oldest drugs used by mankind, as hallucinogens naturally occur in mushrooms, cacti, and various other plants. Various cultures have endorsed their use in medicine, religion and recreation to varying extents, and some have regulated or outright prohibited them. Today, in most countries, possessing many hallucinogens is considered a crime and punished by fines, imprisonment, or even death. In the United States, some deference is given to traditional religious use by members of ethnic minorities such as the Native American Church. Although natural hallucinogenic drugs have been known to mankind for millennia, it was not until the early 20th century that they received extensive attention from Western science. Earlier beginnings include scientific studies of nitrous oxide in the late 18th century and initial studies of the constituents of the peyote cactus in the late 19th century. Starting in 1927 with Kurt Beringer's Der Meskalinrausch (The Mescaline Intoxication), more intensive effort began to be focused on studies of psychoactive plants. Around the same time, Louis Lewin published Phantastica, an extensive survey of psychoactive plants. Important developments in following years included the re-discovery of Mexican magic mushrooms in 1936 by Robert J. Weitlaner and ololiuhqui in 1939 by Richard Evans Schultes. Arguably the most important pre-World War II development was by Albert Hofmann's 1938 invention of the semi-synthetic drug LSD, later discovered to produce hallucinogenic effects, in 1943.

After World War II

After World War II there was an explosion of interest in hallucinogenic drugs in psychiatry, mainly because of the discovery of LSD. Interest in the drugs tended to focus on either the potential for psychotherapeutic applications of the drugs, or on the use of hallucinogens to produce a "controlled psychosis", in order to understand psychotic disorders such as schizophrenia. Hallucinogens were also researched in several countries for their potential as agents of chemical warfare. Most famously, several tragic incidents associated with the CIA's MK-ULTRA mind control research project have been the topic of media attention and lawsuits. At the beginning of the 1950s, the existence of hallucinogenic drugs was virtually unknown among the general public of the West. This soon changed, however, as several influential figures were introduced to the hallucinogenic experience. Aldous Huxley's 1953 essay "The Doors of Perception," describing his experiences with mescaline, and R. Gordon Wasson's 1957 Life magazine article "Seeking the Magic Mushroom" brought the topic into the public limelight. In the early 1960s, counterculture icons such as Jerry Garcia, Timothy Leary, Allen Ginsberg and Ken Kesey advocated the drugs for their psychedelic effects, and a large subculture of drug users was spawned. Psychedelic drugs played a major role in catalyzing the vast social changes initiated in the 1960s. As a result of the growing popularity of LSD and disdain for the hippies with whom it was heavily associated, LSD was banned in the United States in 1967.

Effects

The following are effects of hallucinogens:
- "Mixes up" the central nervous system, speeds things up and then slows things down randomly.
- Distorts messages within the brain, and this can be felt as a distortion in perception. Can cause hallucinations.
- Milder hallucinogens are experienced as an enhancement of the senses: more sensitive to touch, pain can be magnified, music sounds better, hearing is altered, and vision can be enhanced or blurred.
- Our perception of time can be affected.

- Thought processes are affected: poor short term memory, alternating inability to focus and enhanced ability to focus, reduced ability to learn, and giddiness.
- Other effects would include increased blood pressure, increased heart rate, and increased appetite.

Cannabis

Cannabis, also known as marijuana or pot, is a commonly used substance abuse drug. When taken, it relaxes the mind and body, affects the mood, and heightens sensory perceptions. Cannabis use speeds up heart rate, dries out the mouth and throat, impairs the ability to react to external stimuli, and causes lethargy. In large doses, cannabis may cause hallucinations and panic attacks. Long-term users of cannabis exhibit decreased motivation and laziness. The general risks of prolonged cannabis use are psychological dependence, impaired memory and cognitive abilities, increased blood pressure, lung cancer, emphysema, impaired coordination, and diminished fertility.

Other Drugs

Steroids

Many people looking to enhance their muscular strength and endurance have foolishly used anabolic steroids, which are synthetic derivatives of the male hormone testosterone. It is true that steroids will rapidly increase muscle strength and endurance, but they also are very bad for the liver, the brain, and the reproductive organs. Individuals who use steroids for a long period of time are more likely to develop heart disease. There are also harmful side effects associated with such steroid alternatives as human growth hormone (HGH) and gamma hydroxybutyrate (GHB). These substances both are known to cause medical complications like nausea, seizures, and even coma.

Anabolic Steroids

Anabolic steroids are synthetically produced variants of the naturally occurring male hormone testosterone. Both males and females have testosterone produced in their bodies: males in the testes, and females in the ovaries and other tissues. The full name for this class of drugs is androgenic (promoting masculine characteristics) anabolic (tissue building) steroids (the class of drugs). Some of the common street (slang) names for anabolic steroids include arnolds, gym candy, pumpers, roids, stackers, weight trainers, and juice. Currently, there are more than 100 different types of anabolic steroids that have been developed, and each requires a prescription to be used legally in the United States.

Federal law placed anabolic steroids in Schedule III of the Controlled Substances Act (CSA) as of February 27, 1991. Arnolds, gym candy, pumpers, roids, stackers, weight trainers, gear, and juice are typical street names for steroids. Anabolic steroid abuse has been associated with a wide range of adverse side effects ranging from some that are physically unattractive, such as acne and breast development in men, to others that are life threatening. Most of the effects are reversible if the abuser stops taking the drug, but some can be permanent. In addition to the physical effects, anabolic steroids can also cause increased irritability and aggression.

Trafficking trends and users: For purposes of illegal use there are several sources; the most common illegal source is from smuggling steroids into the United States from other countries such as Mexico and European countries. Smuggling from these areas is easier because a prescription is not required for the purchase of steroids. Less often steroids found in the illicit market are diverted from legitimate sources (e.g. thefts or inappropriate prescribing) or produced in clandestine laboratories. Results from the 2005 Monitoring the Future Study, which surveys students in eighth, tenth, and twelfth grades, show that 1.7% of eighth graders, 2.0% of tenth graders, and 2.6% of twelfth graders reported using steroids at least once in their lifetimes. Regarding the ease by which one can obtain steroids, 18.1% of eighth graders, 29.7% of tenth graders, and 39.7% of twelfth graders surveyed in 2005 reported that steroids were "fairly easy" or "very easy" to obtain. During 2005 56.8% of twelfth graders surveyed reported that using steroids was a "great risk." The Centers for Disease Control and Prevention (CDC) also conducts a survey of high school students throughout the United States, the Youth Risk Behavior Surveillance System (YRBSS) 4.8% of all high school students surveyed by CDC in 2005 reported lifetime use of steroid pills/shots without a doctor's prescription.

Administration

Anabolic steroids can be taken orally, injected intramuscularly, or rubbed on the skin when in the form of gels or creams. These drugs are often used in patterns called cycling, which involves taking multiple doses of steroids over a specific period of time, stopping for a period, and starting again. Users also frequently combine several different types of steroids in a process known as stacking. By doing this, users believe that the different steroids will interact to produce an effect on muscle size that is greater than the effects of using each drug individually. Another mode of steroid use is called "pyramiding." With this method users slowly escalate steroid use (increasing the number of drugs used at one time and/or the dose and frequency of one or more steroids), reach a peak amount at mid-cycle and gradually taper the dose toward the end of the cycle. The escalation of steroid use can vary with different types of training. Body builders and weight lifters tend to escalate their dose to a much higher level than do long distance runners or swimmers.

Long term effects

From case reports, the incidence of life-threatening effects appears to be low, but serious adverse effects may be under-recognized or under-reported. Data from animal studies seem to support this possibility. One study found that exposing male mice for one-fifth of their lifespan to steroid doses comparable to those taken by human athletes caused a high percentage of premature deaths. Steroid abuse has been associated with cardiovascular diseases (CVD), including heart attacks and strokes, even in athletes younger than 30. Steroids contribute to the development of CVD, partly by changing the levels of lipoproteins that carry cholesterol in the blood. Steroids, particularly the oral types, increase the level of low-density lipoprotein (LDL) and decrease the level of high-density lipoprotein (HDL). High LDL and low HDL levels increase the risk of atherosclerosis, a condition in which fatty substances are deposited inside arteries and disrupt blood flow. If blood is prevented from reaching the heart, the result can be a heart attack. If blood is prevented from reaching the brain, the result can be a stroke. Steroids also increase the risk that blood clots will form in blood vessels, potentially disrupting blood flow and damaging the heart muscle so that it does not pump blood effectively.

Over-the-counter drugs

In the United States, there are more than half a million health products that can be purchased without the approval of a doctor. Many of these over-the–counter drugs

(OCD) (aspirin, for example) can have serious side effects. Some drugs that were obtained only with a doctor's permission in the past are now available for immediate purchase. Consumers should be aware that OCD products carry possible dangers. Nasal sprays, for instance, can have the opposite effect of what was intended if they are used too often. Laxatives can also do permanent damage to the body if they are taken too regularly. Eye drops may eventually make eyes redder if they are used habitually. Lastly, OCD sleep aids have not yet been adequately researched, and some doctors suspect they may have negative consequences for mental health.

Analgesics

An analgesic (known as a painkiller) is any member of the diverse group of drugs used to relieve pain (achieve analgesia). Analgesic drugs act in various ways on the peripheral and central nervous systems; they include paracetamol (acetaminophen), the nonsteroidal anti-inflammatory drugs (NSAIDs) such as the salicylates, narcotic drugs such as morphine, synthetic drugs with narcotic properties such as tramadol, and various others. Some other classes of drugs not normally considered analgesics are used to treat neuropathic pain syndromes; these include tricyclic antidepressants and anticonvulsants.

Aspirin and NSAIDS

The exact mechanism of action of paracetamol/acetaminophen is uncertain, but it appears to be acting centrally. Aspirin and the other NSAIDs inhibit cyclooxygenase, leading to a decrease in prostaglandin production; this reduces pain and also inflammation (in contrast to paracetamol and the opioids).
Paracetamol has few side effects, but dosing is limited by possible hepatotoxicity (potential for liver damage). NSAIDs may predispose to peptic ulcers, renal failure, allergic reactions, and hearing loss. They may also increase the risk of hemorrhage

by affecting platelet function. The use of certain NSAIDs in children under 16 suffering from viral illness may contribute to Reye's syndrome.

Topical analgesics

Topical analgesia is generally recommended to avoid systemic side-effects. Painful joints, for example, may be treated with an ibuprofen- or diclofenac-containing gel; capsaicin also is used topically. Lidocaine, an anesthetic, and steroids may be injected into painful joints for longer-term pain relief. Lidocaine is also used for painful mouth sores and to numb areas for dental work and minor medical procedures.

Treatment for chronic or neuropathic pain

In patients with chronic or neuropathic pain, various other substances may have analgesic properties. Tricyclic antidepressants, especially amitriptyline, have been shown to improve pain in what appears to be a central manner. The exact mechanism of carbamazepine, gabapentin and pregabalin is similarly unclear, but these anticonvulsants are used to treat neuropathic pain with modest success.

Psychotropic agents

Psychotropic agents, including Tetrahydrocannabinol (THC) and some other cannabinoids, either from the Cannabis sativa plant or synthetic, have analgesic properties, although the use of cannabis derivatives is illegal in many countries. Other psychotropic analgesic agents include ketamine (an NMDA receptor antagonist), clonidine and other α2-adrenoreceptor agonists, and mexiletine and other local anesthetic analogues.

Psychological effects of prescription drugs

Sometimes, it is more difficult for patients to notice the psychological effects of a prescription medication than the physical side effects. The drugs most likely to cause noticeable psychological problems are those for depression, high blood pressure, epilepsy, asthma, insomnia, and arthritis. Doctors assert that psychological problems associate with drugs are more likely to affect people as they get older, especially if they are taking a large number of medications. Many of these drugs either induce depression by slowing the blood pressure, or induce anxiety by overstimulating the nervous system. The best way to manage to psychological side effects of a prescription drug is to learn as much as possible about the drug and closely monitor yourself in consultation with a doctor.

Inhalants

Inhalants are a diverse group of substances that include volatile solvents, gases, and nitrites that are sniffed, snorted, huffed, or bagged to produce intoxicating effects similar to alcohol. These substances are found in common household products like glues, lighter fluid, cleaning fluids, and paint products. Inhalant abuse is the deliberate inhaling or sniffing of these substances to get high, and it is estimated that about 1,000 substances are misused in this manner. The easy accessibility, low cost, legal status, and ease of transport and concealment make inhalants one of the first substances abused by children. Inhalants are not regulated under the Controlled Substances Act (CSA).

Categories
There are four general categories of inhalants:
- Volatile solvents are liquids that vaporize at room temperatures. They are found in a multitude of inexpensive, easily available products used for common household and industrial purposes. These include paint thinners

- 128 -

and removers, dry-cleaning fluids, degreasers, gasoline, glues, correction fluids, and felt-tip marker fluids.

- Aerosols are sprays that contain propellants and solvents. They include spray paints, deodorant and hair sprays, vegetable oil sprays for cooking, and fabric protectors.

- Gases include medical anesthetics as well as gases used in household or commercial products. Nitrous oxide is the most abused of these gases and can be found in whipped cream dispensers. Household or commercial products containing gases include butane lighters, propane tanks, whipped cream dispensers, and refrigerants.

Nitrites often are considered a special class of inhalants. Unlike most other inhalants, which act directly on the CNS, nitrites act as vasodilators and muscle relaxers. While other inhalants are used to alter mood, nitrites are used primarily as sexual enhancers. These are commonly known as "poppers" or "snappers," and were prescribed in the past to treat some patients for heart pain. While technically illegal, they are easily purchased under re-purposed forms.

Street names

Some street names for inhalants are:

Air blast	Moon gas
Ames	Oz
Amys	Pearls
Aroma of men	Poor man's pot
Bolt	Poppers
Boppers	Quicksilver
Bullet	Rush Snappers
Bullet bolt	Satan's secret
Buzz bomb	Shoot the breeze
Discorama	Snappers

Hardware	Snotballs
Heart-on	Spray
Hiagra in a bottle	Texas shoe shine
Highball	Thrust
Hippie crack	Toilet water
Huff	Toncho
Laughing gas	Whippets
Locker room	Whiteout

Short term effects

Most inhalants act directly on the central nervous system (CNS) to produce psychoactive, or mind-altering, effects. They have short-term effects similar to anesthetics, which slow the body's functions. Inhaled chemicals are rapidly absorbed through the lungs into the bloodstream and quickly distributed to the brain and other organs. Within seconds of inhalation, the user experiences intoxication along with other effects similar to those produced by alcohol. Alcohol-like effects may include slurred speech, an inability to coordinate movements, euphoria, and dizziness. In addition, users may experience lightheadedness, hallucinations, and delusions. Inhalants have been blamed for involuntary eye movements, nausea, lethargy, impaired motor skills, nosebleeds, loss of appetite, aggressiveness, and an increased risk of accident and injury. The effects of inhalants typically only last for a period of seconds. Prolonged sniffing of the highly concentrated chemicals in solvents or aerosol sprays can induce irregular and rapid heart rhythms and lead to heart failure and death within minutes of a session of prolonged sniffing. It is quite possible to die the first time you ever try an inhalant. This syndrome, known as "sudden sniffing death," can result from a single session of inhalant use.

Long term effects

Chronic exposure to inhalants can produce significant, sometimes irreversible, damage to the heart, lungs, liver, and kidneys as well as lead to hepatitis, kidney failure, respiratory trouble, irregular heartbeat, bone problems, and heart failure. The chronic use of inhalants has been associated with a number of serious health problems. Sniffing glue and paint thinner causes kidney abnormalities, while sniffing the solvents toluene and trichloroethylene cause liver damage. Memory impairment, attention deficits, and diminished non-verbal intelligence have been related to the abuse of inhalants. Deaths resulting from heart failure, asphyxiation, or aspiration have occurred. A strong need to continue using inhalants has been reported among many individuals, particularly those who abuse inhalants for prolonged periods over many days. Compulsive use and a mild withdrawal syndrome can occur with long-term inhalant abuse. Additional symptoms exhibited by long-term inhalant abusers include weight loss, muscle weakness, disorientation, inattentiveness, lack of coordination, irritability, and depression.

Use and user population

Among students surveyed as part of the 2005 Monitoring the Future study, 17.1% of eighth graders, 13.1% of tenth graders, and 11.4% of twelfth graders reported lifetime use of inhalants. Approximately 37.5% of eighth graders and 45.7% of tenth graders surveyed in 2005 reported that trying inhalants once or twice was a "great risk." The Centers for Disease Control and Prevention (CDC) also conducts a survey of high school students throughout the United States called the Youth Risk Behavior Surveillance System (YRBSS). Among students surveyed for the 2005 YRBSS, 12.4% reported using inhalants at least one time during their lifetime.

Legislation

Although not regulated under the Controlled Substances Act (CSA), many state legislatures have attempted to deter youth who buy legal products to get high by placing restrictions on the sale of these products to minors. As reported by the National Conference of State Legislatures, by 2000, 38 States had adopted laws preventing the sale, use, and/or distribution to minors of various products commonly abused as inhalants. Some States have introduced fines, incarceration, or mandatory treatment for the sale, distribution, use, and/or possession of inhalable chemicals.

Predatory drugs

Rohypnol, Ketamine, and GHB and its analogues GBL, and BD 1,4 have gained notoriety as drugs used to facilitate sexual assault, adding an urgency to law enforcement efforts to pursue traffickers of these drugs. These drugs render the victim incapable of resisting sexual advances. Sexual Assaults facilitated by these drugs can be difficult to prosecute or even recognize because:

- Victims may not be aware that they ingested a drug at all. The drugs are invisible and odorless when dissolved in water. They are somewhat salty tasting, but are indiscernible when dissolved in beverages such as sodas, juice, liquor, or beer.
- Due to memory problems induced by these drugs, the victim may not be aware of the attack until 8-12 hours after it occurred.
- The drugs are metabolized quickly, so there may be little physical evidence to support the claim that the drugs were used to facilitate an assault.
- Memory impairment caused by the drugs also eliminates evidence about the attack.

Anorectic drugs

A number of drugs have been developed and marketed to replace amphetamines as appetite suppressants. These anorectic drugs include benzphetamine (Didrex®), diethylproprion (Tenuate®, Tepanil®), mazindol (Sanorex®, Mazanor®), phendimetrazine (Bontril®, Prelu-27®), and phentermine (lonamin®, Fastin®, Adipex®). These substances are in Schedule III or IV of the CSA and produce some amphetamine-like effects. Of these diet pills, phentermine is the most widely prescribed and most frequently encountered on the illicit market. Two Schedule IV anorectics often used in combination with phentermine (phen-fen combo), fenfluramine and dexfenfluramine, were removed from the U.S. market due to heart valve problems.

Generic drugs

When doctors refer to the generic name of a drug, they are referring to a shortened version of the drug's exact chemical name. A particular drug may be sold under a variety of different brand names (trade names chosen by each manufacturer). When a brand name drug has lost its patent protection, a competing manufacturer copies the original drug and markets a generic version. It costs a great deal less than the brand name form of the drug. .Since most of the time, there is no substantial difference between the brand-name version of a drug and its generic counterpart, patients will save money by selecting the generic version. Patients should confer with their doctors about any changes that have occurred after starting a new medication to ensure that the prescribed dose is appropriate. It is also important that the patient learn how to store particular medications so that they do not diminish in effectiveness or become contaminated.

Prescription drugs

Every year, the Food and Drug Administration of the United States (FDA) grants permission for the production of about twenty new prescription drugs. Although these drugs can be very beneficial, they are frequently misused. The most common mistakes associated with prescription drug use are overdosing, underdosing, omitting labeling information, ordering the wrong dose form (liquid instead of solid, for instance), and neglecting to recognize an allergic reaction to a drug. Failure to properly take a prescription medication can lead to recurrent infections, medical complications, and, even, death. Some patients endanger their own health by failing to adhere to the dosage schedule or failing to tell their doctor about side effects.

<u>Physical side effects</u>

There is no prescription drug that does not cause side effects, even if these go unnoticed by the patient. It is very common to have an allergic reaction to a drug. Patients frequently develop allergic reactions to penicillin and other antibiotics. These allergic responses may cause nausea, hives, a drop in blood pressure, constriction of the breathing passages, and even collapse. Patients who suffer an extreme reaction may require an immediate injection of adrenaline to maintain their vital processes. With other drugs, complications can include heart problems, blood disorders, birth defects, blindness, and memory problems. For these reasons, prescription drugs should only be taken under the close supervision of a doctor.

Psychotherapeutics

Some people have disorders that are caused by an imbalance in the chemical neurotransmitters in the brain. These powerful drugs correct the imbalance and allow those who need them to function normally. An example is Chlorpromazine, also known as CPZ. These drugs are seldom abused because the effect on a normally functioning brain is not perceived as pleasant. There are also powerful side effects to these drugs and usually other drugs are prescribed to be taken with them to control the side effects. These side effects are usually unpleasant enough to stop anyone abusing the drug from trying it again.

Psychiatric medication

Many doctors complain that patients have become too reliant on the "quick fix" promised by psychiatric drugs, and are unwilling to take the behavioral steps necessary to permanently improve their condition. Moreover, many patients fail to get valuable information about the drugs that have been prescribed to them. For instance, a patient should always know why a particular medication is prescribed rather than another, and what specific symptoms the medication is designed to treat. A patient should be aware of the potential side effects of any medication, and should know how long it will take for the drug to take effect. As with any medication, a patient should know whether it has dangerous effects when mixed with alcohol or another drug, and he or she should have a clear understanding of how long the drug will have to be taken.

Psychiatric drug therapy

Psychiatric drugs are those that affect the chemistry of the brain and relieve the symptoms of mental disorder and illness. In recent years, research has produced a generation of extremely safe and effective psychiatric drugs that can help individuals with problems ranging from minor depression to schizophrenia. One of the most common types of drugs is a serotonin boosting medication that is used to treat obsessive compulsive disorder, attention deficit disorder, and depression. Patients should know, however, that it often takes several weeks for psychiatric medications to begin showing results. Also, they should be made aware that these drugs have side effects, some of which are very serious. Psychiatric drugs may continue to be operative after the individual stops taking them.

<u>Drug abuse/substance abuse</u>

Substance abuse is sometimes used as a synonym for drug abuse, drug addiction, and chemical dependency, but actually refers to the use of substances in a manner outside socio-cultural conventions. All use of illicit drugs and all use of licit drugs in a manner not dictated by convention (e.g. according to physician's orders or societal norms) is abuse according to this definition, however there is no universally accepted definition of substance abuse.

Prevention/Treatment

Treatment

Drug addiction is a complex but treatable brain disease. It is characterized by compulsive drug craving, seeking, and use that persist even in the face of severe adverse consequences. For many people, drug addiction becomes chronic, with relapses possible even after long periods of abstinence. In fact, relapse to drug abuse occurs at rates similar to those for other well-characterized, chronic medical illnesses such as diabetes, hypertension, and asthma. As a chronic, recurring illness, addiction may require repeated treatments to increase the intervals between relapses and diminish their intensity, until abstinence is achieved. Through treatment tailored to individual needs, people with drug addiction can recover and lead productive lives. The ultimate goal of drug addiction treatment is to enable an individual to achieve lasting abstinence, but the immediate goals are to reduce drug abuse, improve the patient's ability to function, and minimize the medical and social complications of drug abuse and addiction. Like people with diabetes or heart disease, people in treatment for drug addiction will need to change behavior to adopt a more healthful lifestyle.

Treatment can help many people change destructive behaviors, avoid relapse, and successfully remove themselves from a life of substance abuse and addiction. This is a long-term process and frequently requires multiple episodes of treatment. Key principles:

- No single treatment is appropriate for all individuals.
- Treatment needs to be readily available.
- Effective treatment attends to multiple needs of the individual, not just his or her drug addiction.

- An individual's treatment plan must be assessed often and modified to meet the person's changing needs.
- An adequate duration of treatment is critical.
- Counseling and other behavioral therapies are critical.
- For certain types of disorders, medications are an important element of treatment, especially alongside therapy.
- Those with coexisting mental disorders should have both disorders treated in an integrated way.
- Medical management of withdrawal syndrome is only the first stage of addiction treatment and by itself does little.
- Treatment does not need to be voluntary to be effective.
- Possible drug use during treatment must be monitored.
- Treatment programs should provide assessment for HIV and other infectious diseases and provide counseling to help patients modify or change risky behaviors.

Most countries have health facilities that specialize in the treatment of drug abuse, although access may be limited to larger population centers and the social taboos regarding drug use may make those who need the medical treatment reluctant to take advantage of it. For example, it is estimated that only fifteen percent of injection drug abusers thought to be in need are receiving treatment. Patients may require acute and long-term maintenance treatment and relapse prevention, complemented by suitable rehabilitation.

Treatments for drug addiction vary widely according to the types of drugs involved, amount of drugs used, duration of the drug addiction, medical complications and the social needs of the individual. Determining the best type of recovery program for an addicted person depends on a number of factors, including: personality, drug(s) of addiction, concept of spirituality or religion, mental or physical illness, and local availability and affordability of programs.

For most drug users, the most difficult part of the recovery process is admitting that they have a problem. Sometimes, it is necessary for friends and family to intervene in order to get the user to realize the dangers of drug use. Once this is accomplished, treatment can take place in an outpatient facility, a residential facility, or a hospital. Many individuals receive both physical and psychological therapy to help them break the addiction in its every form. For drugs that have painful withdrawal effects, it is recommended that the user be supervised closely by an appropriately trained person. One of the key parts of any rehabilitation effort is continued contact with the patient after the period of therapy ends; most addicts relapse into their former behaviors after completing therapy, and additional treatment may be appropriate.

Abstinence based and medical based treatments

Abstinence-based approaches set as a goal complete abstinence from all addictive substances, including both licit and illicit, prescribed and unprescribed. While the harm-reduction approach has been demonstrated to work well with opioids, the abstinence-based approach is the medical community standard of care for sedative (including alcohol) dependence.

Beyond the sociological issues, many drugs of abuse can lead to addiction, chemical dependency, or adverse health effects, such as lung cancer or emphysema from cigarette smoking. Medical treatment therefore centers on two aspects: 1) breaking the addiction, 2) treating the health problems.

Pharmacotherapy

The development of pharmacotherapies for drug dependency treatment is currently in progress. New immunotherapies that prevent drugs like cocaine, methamphetamine, phencyclidine, nicotine, and opioids from reaching the brain are in the early stages of testing as is ibogaine, an alkaloid found in the Tabernanthe iboga plant of West Central Africa. Medications such as Buprenorphine, which block the drugs active site in the brain, are another new option for the treatment of opioid addiction. Depot forms of medications, which require only weekly or monthly dosing, are also under investigation. Traditionally, new pharmacotherapies are quickly adopted in primary care settings; however, drugs for substance abuse treatment have faced many barriers. Naltrexone, a drug originally marketed under the name "ReVia," and now marketed in intramuscular formulation as "Vivitrol" or in oral formulation as a generic, is a medication approved for the treatment of alcohol dependence. This drug has reached very few patients. This may be due to a number of factors, including resistance by Addiction Medicine specialists and lack of resources.

Alcohol addiction: Some pharmacological treatments for alcohol addiction include drugs like disulfiram, acamprosate and topiramate, but rather than substituting for alcohol, these drugs are intended to reduce the desire to drink, either by directly reducing cravings as with acamprosate and topiramate, or by producing unpleasant effects when alcohol is consumed, as with disulfiram. These drugs can be effective if treatment is maintained, but compliance can be an issue as alcoholic patients often forget to take their medication, or discontinue use because of excessive side effects. Additional drugs acting on glutamate neurotransmission such as modafinil, lamotrigine, gabapentin and memantine have also been proposed for use in treating addiction to alcohol and other drugs. Opioid antagonists such as naltrexone and nalmefene have also been used successfully in the treatment of alcohol addiction, which is often particularly challenging to treat. These drugs have also been used to a lesser extent for long-term maintenance treatment of former opiate addicts, but cannot be started until the patient has been abstinent for an extended period; otherwise they can trigger acute opioid withdrawal symptoms.

Nicotine addiction: Another area in which drug treatment has been widely used is in the treatment of nicotine addiction. Various drugs have been used for this purpose such as bupropion, mecamylamine and the more recently developed varenicline.

The cannabinoid antagonist rimonabant has also been tested for treatment of nicotine addiction but has not been widely adopted for this purpose.

Stimulant addiction: Treatment of stimulant addiction can often be difficult, with substitute drugs often being ineffective, although newer drugs such as nocaine, vanoxerine and modafinil may have more promise in this area, as well as the GABAB agonist baclofen. Another strategy that has recently been through successful trials used a combination of the benzodiazepine antagonist flumazenil with hydroxyzine and gabapentin for the treatment of methamphetamine addiction.

Anti-addictive drugs: Other forms of treatment include replacement drugs such as methadone or buprenorphine, used as a substitute for illicit opiate drugs. Although these drugs are themselves addictive, opioid dependency is often so strong that a way to stabilize levels of opioid needed and a way to gradually reduce the levels of opioid needed are required. Substitute drugs for other forms of drug dependence have historically been less successful than opioid substitute treatment, but some limited success has been seen with drugs such as dexamphetamine to treat stimulant addiction, and clomethiazole to treat alcohol addiction.

Controversial treatments: Ibogaine is a psychoactive drug that specifically interrupts the addictive response, and is currently being studied for its effects upon cocaine, heroin, nicotine, and SSRI addicts. Alternative medicine clinics offering ibogaine treatment have appeared along the U.S. border. Ibogaine treatment for drug addiction can be reasonably effective, but potentially dangerous side effects which have been linked to several deaths have limited its adoption by conventional medical practice. A synthetic analogue of ibogaine, 18-methoxycoronaridine has also been developed which has similar efficacy but less side effects, however this drug is still being tested in animals and human trials have not yet been carried out.

Residential drug treatment and 12 step programs

Residential drug treatment can be broadly divided into two camps: 12 step programs or Therapeutic Communities. 12 step programs have the advantage of coming with an instant social support network though some find the spiritual context not to their taste. Other programs may use Cognitive-Behavioral Therapy an approach that looks at the relationship between thoughts feelings and behaviors, recognizing that a change in any of these areas can affect the whole. CBT sees addiction as a behavior rather than a disease and subsequently curable, or rather, unlearnable. CBT programs recognize that for some individuals controlled use is a more realistic possibility.

One of many recovery methods is the 12 step recovery program, with prominent examples including Alcoholics Anonymous and Narcotics Anonymous. They are commonly known and used for a variety of addictions for the individual addicted and the family of the individual. Substance-abuse rehabilitation (or "rehab") centers frequently offer a residential treatment program for the seriously addicted in order to isolate the patient from drugs and interactions with other users and dealers. Outpatient clinics usually offer a combination of individual counseling and group counseling. Frequently a physician or psychiatrist will assist with prescriptions to assist with the side effects of the addiction (the most common side effect that the medications can help is anxiety).

Though it was first introduced by Alcoholics Anonymous, the twelve-step method of recovery has become the model for rehabilitation in over 200 organizations. The basic tenet of a twelve-step program is that the user is powerless to control his or her own addiction. In order to be a part of the program, the individual must want to quit. Then, he or she will get in touch with a group and attend meetings. One of the fundamental parts of the twelve-step program is the cooperation among members; when one feels tempted to relapse into the former behavior, he or she is supposed to call on other members for support. Individuals are ultimately responsible for themselves, however, and are not required to pay dues or to attend any meeting if they do not desire.

Outpatient treatment centers

Many procedures that at one time required overnight hospitalization can now be performed at outpatient centers. Outpatient centers can be freestanding and self-sustaining, or they can be affiliated with a larger medical center. Outpatient centers have become the preferred place to get a tonsillectomy, cataract removal, breast biopsy, vasectomy, or plastic surgery procedure. Because they have much lower overhead costs, outpatient facilities are able to provide services for a fraction of the cost for a similar procedure at a hospital. For this reason, insurance companies encourage their clients to have minor surgery performed at outpatient centers. A popular spin-off of the outpatient treatment center is the freestanding emergency center, where people can receive treatment for minor illness or injury in a somewhat shorter amount of time.

Alternative therapies

Alternative therapies, such as acupuncture, are used by some practitioners to alleviate the symptoms of drug addiction. In 1997, the American Medical Association (AMA) was adopted as policy following statement after a report on a number of alternative therapies including acupuncture:

There is little evidence to confirm the safety or efficacy of most alternative therapies. Much of the information currently known about these therapies makes it clear that many have not been shown to be efficacious. Well-designed, stringently controlled research should be done to evaluate the efficacy of alternative therapies. Acupuncture has been shown to be no more effective than control treatments in the treatment of opiate dependence. Acupuncture, acupressure, laser therapy and electrostimulation have no demonstrated efficacy for smoking cessation.

<u>Successful outcome</u>

Many different ideas circulate regarding what is considered a "successful" outcome in the recovery from addiction. It has widely been established that abstinence from addictive substances is generally accepted as a "successful" outcome; however differences of opinion exist as to the extent of abstinence required. In the USA, the goal of treatment for drug dependence is generally total abstinence from all drugs, which while theoretically the ideal outcome, is in practice often very difficult to achieve.

Harm reduction strategies

One alternative involves replacing failed law enforcement policies with harm-reduction strategies, which focus on reducing the societal costs of drug abuse and other drug use. Techniques include education to avoid overdose, needle exchange programs to reduce the spread of blood-borne diseases, and opioid substitution therapy to reduce crime related to the procurement of drugs. This pragmatic approach is known as the harm reduction paradigm. Harm reduction also addresses special populations, such as drug-using parents, pregnant drug users and users with psychiatric comorbidity. The philosophy of harm reduction accepts that drug use is part of the community, but that it must be addressed as a public health issue rather than a criminal one. Harm-reduction measures are at odds with the prevailing framework of international drug control, which rests on law enforcement and the criminalization of behaviors related to illicit drug use. However, harm-reduction has had a notable impact and is slowly gaining popularity.

Hospitals

There are several different kinds of hospitals. Private (or community) hospitals are those that have between 50 and 400 beds and provide more personalized care than do public hospitals. Private hospitals may be run either for profit or as a nonprofit business. In public hospitals, the care is administered by the health service of the city, county, military, or Veterans Administration. Whereas the quality of care in a private hospital is determined by the skill of the doctors, the quality of care in a public hospital is more dependent on the general state of the institution that runs it. In the United States, there are approximately 300 hospitals that are directly affiliated with university medical schools. These hospitals often offer the most advanced treatments because the doctors there are required to stay abreast of all developments in their respective fields.

If you have the time, it is a good idea to compare various hospitals before determining where to receive treatment. One easy way to collect information is to ask your doctors which hospitals they would recommend, and why. Another way to evaluate hospitals is to inquire about the ratio of nurses to patients; many hospitals that are trying to cut costs provide fewer than the standard number of nurses. If you are having a rare procedure performed, you should ask whether the hospital has performed the procedure recently and what their success rate has been. If it is possible to do so, you should tour the various hospitals, checking to ensure that they are clean and orderly and have a courteous staff.

The most expensive form of health care is inpatient health care at a hospital. Because it is so expensive, many insurance companies require conclusive proof that inpatient treatment is necessary before they will pay for it. Patients should be on the lookout for insurance companies that pay for treatment on the basis of diagnostic-related groups (DRGs): this means that the insurance company pays a flat fee for a certain kind of procedure, and so the hospital can make money if they can provide the service at a cheaper cost. Emergency room visits can also be very expensive, and they should only be made when absolutely necessary. Most of the time, patients who are not in dire need of help will wait for a long time in an emergency room and will be presented with a large bill, which may not be covered by their health insurance.

Breaking the addictive process

Stopping outright is necessary to treat the disease of addiction and ensure the patient's survival. However, drug addicts are not likely to begin fighting to save themselves until those around them permit the addicts to feel the full force of their harmful choices. In real addictive behaviors the bottoms keep coming, even deeper, until the addicted person dies or learns that life cannot continue without real change. Intervention is needed; the addict is totally committed to the addictive process and will not be able to break this cycle without some form of intervention. Addicts rarely enter treatment without pressure because, from their point of view, treatment means having to give up the one thing that is most important to them. Addiction is not a self-curing disease. Addicts cannot learn or think their way out of it. Recovery is not part of the disease that addiction is. It does not just happen; it requires a plan and hard work. Screening for drug use followed by immediate intervention and, if necessary, referral to treatment, are keys to ensuring drug users' long-term health. And as with all progressive diseases of a catastrophic nature, earlier diagnosis and treatment produce better outcomes. In order to solve one's drug problems, one would have to stop all abused drugs—for example, not only marijuana but also cigarettes and alcohol consumption. Detoxification is only the beginning of the solution for drug addiction.

Detoxification

Whenever an individual with an alcohol problem begins treatment, the first step is detoxification, or the gradual removal of alcohol from the system. Most of the time, detoxification does not produce major withdrawal symptoms. However, those who have been drinking heavily for a long period may develop severe symptoms, including seizures and delirium tremens (also known as DTs). Delirium tremens is a condition in which the individual becomes agitated, and may have delusions, a rapid heartbeat, sweating, vivid hallucinations, fever, and trembling hands. This condition is most likely to strike those alcoholics who also suffer from malnutrition, depression, or fatigue, and usually ceases after a few alcohol-free days.

Redirecting the addictive process

Detoxification is only the beginning of the solution for drug addiction: Recovery is not only about not acting out; it is also about redirecting the addictive process. Addicts must not only break off their relationship with addictive substances or events and take the necessary steps to transform their addictive attitudes, beliefs, values and behaviors. Addicts must give their brain the time to readjust to the absence of drugs and then learn behaviors that will allow them to stay off drugs. If people don't claim and redirect their pleasure-centered or power-centered impulses, they may return to some other deviant form of acting out. They will find another substance or event that helps them achieve the trance. Or, they may become a "dry drunk" – they have stopped drinking but have not surrendered their addictive personalities. Addicts are not relaxed or happy with their drug(s) deprivation, but rather they are resentful and angry. Addicts often ask:" Other people can drink and use drugs. Why can't I?" These episodes of white-knuckle sobriety are not part of recovery; they are part of the active disease of addiction.

Psychotherapy

Detoxification, followed by psychotherapy and/or attendance to self help groups such as NA, is the key to recovery. Psychotherapy, treating the underlying cause of drug abuse, can only be successful in people being free of intoxication and having a clear head. A brain high on drugs is a brain that is dysfunctional. Addicts only need to think about today, about taking care of recovery one day at a time. The longer an addicted person stays in treatment, the better that person does over the long-term. Recovery is about allowing drug users to feel guilt. Guilt means we have committed an action that was wrong or not helpful to others or to ourselves. Many people, therefore, enter recovery with a deep sense of shame. These people enter a period of deep shamefulness as they look more honestly at their past actions.

Psychotherapy refers to a broad spectrum of counseling techniques based on conversation between a trained professional and an individual seeking help. Most mental health professionals are trained in a few different psychotherapeutic styles and can tailor their approach to the patient's needs. Progress in psychotherapy can at times be difficult to measure, and insurance companies have grown increasingly unwilling to pay for long treatments. For this reason, many individuals seek psychotherapy for a specific problem or to correct a specific feeling or behavior. Most people find that the process of talking and listening is therapeutic in itself and allows them to discover solutions to their problems that were unavailable through reflection alone.

Psychodynamic psychotherapy

Most practicing psychotherapists take a dynamic view of mental health; that is, they believe that the individual's unconscious life and experiences during his or her formative years have a tremendous influence on his or her adult behavior. Psychodynamic treatment is often quite brief, and usually is aimed at stopping a particular behavior. Scientific evidence has emerged that suggests that psychodynamic psychotherapy can actually rewire the brain in a matter of weeks, so that the target behavior or feeling becomes habitual. This kind of therapy is often the best option for otherwise high-functioning adults who have experienced a recurring problem or trouble in a particular situation.

Cognitive-behavioral therapy

Cognitive-behavioral therapy is designed to help individuals break out of bad or disordered habits of thought and behavior. In cognitive therapy, the therapist helps the individual identify his or her central beliefs, recognize potentially negative

Copyright © Mometrix Media. You have been licensed one copy of this document for personal use only. Any other reproduction or redistribution is strictly prohibited. All rights reserved.

thought patterns, and learn new ways of thinking and approaching problems. Cognitive therapy has most clearly benefited individuals suffering from major depression or anxiety disorders. Behavior therapy follows a similar course, except that it aims to replace problematic behaviors rather than thoughts. Many therapists believe that changing a person's behavior will naturally change his or her thoughts or emotions. Behavior therapy seems to work best when a patient is crippled by a specific habit, for instance alcoholism, drug abuse, or a phobia.

Alcoholism

Inpatient and outpatient treatment

For a long time, a four-week stay at a psychiatric hospital or residential facility was considered necessary for a recovering alcoholic. This inpatient treatment was usually successful, too: over 70% of those who completed such a treatment were sober for five years afterward, according to one study. Unfortunately, inpatient treatment is expensive, and insurance companies have been increasingly unwilling to pay for it. So, outpatient treatments like group therapy, family therapy, interventions, and organizations like Alcoholics Anonymous have become more popular in recent years. Some studies have indicated that intensive outpatient treatment can be as effective as inpatient care, especially if the individual continues it for at least a year.

Treatment medications

If alcoholism is caught in its early stages, doctors often prescribe antidepressant or antianxiety medication. These drugs increase the amount of serotonin in the brain and are believed to reduce painful cravings for alcohol. Doctors also recommend that recovering alcoholics take vitamin supplements to remedy the malnutrition that prolonged alcoholism may cause. For especially severe cases, doctors may prescribe Antabuse (the commercial name for the drug disulfiram), which causes an individual to become nauseous or ill when they consume alcohol. Individuals on this medication must also be careful to avoid foods that have been marinated or cooked in alcohol; indeed, some sensitive individuals may even have an adverse reaction to the alcohol in shaving lotion. Although Antabuse is effective in forcing an individual to stop drinking, it does not treat any of the psychological or social causes of drinking.

Brief interventions and moderation training

Brief interventions are short, intense training sessions that teach alcoholics the skills they will need to battle their drinking problem. These programs, which typically last about 8 weeks and center on topics like "assertiveness" and "self-esteem," are best suited for individuals who do not have a physical dependence on alcohol. Moderation training, another form of treatment, tries to equip drinkers with the skills to manage their drinking, by showing them ways to reduce consumption and avoid problematic situations. This method is somewhat controversial because critics assert that the only good choice for chronic alcohol abusers is abstinence. However, advocates of moderation training point out that their programs are designed for less severe cases and that their goals are more realistic than those found in other programs.

AA

The most famous self-help program for individuals battling a drinking problem is Alcoholics Anonymous (AA). This global organization seeks to force alcoholics to admit their problems and to rely on one another for support in solving them. Every member of AA will have a "sponsor," another member whom they can call upon if they are tempted to drink. AA also features a 12-step program in which members are forced to take responsibility, to own up to the problems that drinking causes, and to ask God for help. The 12-step model devised by AA has been used in many other self-help organizations. There are other self-help groups, such as Rational Recovery, that adhere to a similar philosophy as AA without the emphasis on spirituality.

Recovery

Defeating alcoholism is often the most difficult challenge an individual will face in his or her lifetime. Relapse into drinking is common; some studies estimate that 90% of recovering alcoholics will drink again within a year after quitting. The people who tend to be successful at abstaining are those who have something to lose: that is, parents of children and people with important jobs. Almost every recovering alcoholic will experience mood swings and an occasional temptation to drink. More and more, relapse prevention is a part of treatment. Relapse prevention involves giving the individual the information and skills to cope with the temptations of alcohol, as well as providing a support network that the individual can rely on in times of stress. Exercise and a general reduction in stress seem to be the most helpful treatment techniques for creating a permanent life away from alcohol.

Relapse prevention

Most substance abusers will relapse several times after kicking the habit. This is important for both the user and the user's support group to know so that they do not become too frustrated at the setbacks on the road to recovery. Some therapists even say that these relapses can strengthen self-understanding and make it more likely that future relapses can be avoided. Over time, substance abusers should be able to recognize the stimuli that make them susceptible to using drugs, and they should learn to avoid these people, places, and situations. It is also important to make the distinction between a minor and a major relapse; often, it is a huge victory for a recovering addict to keep a minor relapse from turning into a major one.

Addicted people remain vulnerable to relapse throughout their lives. Drugs permanently alter the brain chemistry making them forever liable to redevelop uncontrolled use quicker than before. Relapse has much to do with the selfish brain's selective memory of the good times associated with the use of drugs and its selective forgetting of the bad times associated with drug use. Relapse is triggered by cues previously paired with substance use, by stress, or by the presence of the drug itself. All of these phenomena are mediated by increased dopamine release, but even more important, by increased glutamate release. If the environment continues to pile stress on a former drug user, he/she will move to a level of susceptibility where he/she will return to uncontrolled addictive use with just one hit of drugs.

Handling stress

Positive coping mechanisms

The various ways that individuals try to adapt and respond positively to the stresses of life are called positive coping mechanisms. These are healthy, mature ways of dealing with problems, and come in four common forms. Sublimation is redirecting any socially-unacceptable drives into more appropriate activities. Turning one's anger into art, for instance, is sublimation. Religiosity is the process in which the individual reconciles hardship as being a part of God's will or some divine plan. Humor, of course, is a very common way of dealing with stress. Altruism is the act of converting a negative experience into a positive one. People afflicted with lung cancer who speak publicly about the dangers of smoking can be said to be turning a bad experience for them into a positive experience for the community.

Mental exercises

There are a few simple exercises that anyone can perform to avoid being overwhelmed by stress. First, you should be able to recognize the symptoms of your stress; for instance, you might develop backaches or nausea when you are stressed out. It can be very helpful to keep a journal, so that you can express your feelings and work on trying to understand why you get stressed and how you can avoid it. It never hurts to rehearse potentially stressful situations before they occur, so that you will be prepared for action. Sometimes it can be helpful to put stressful situations in perspective: ask yourself if the current problem is likely to seem such a big deal in a week, a month, or a year.

Time management

The failure to manage time effectively can be one of the most common sources of stress in contemporary society. Some common symptoms of poor time management are a feeling of rushing, the chronic inability to make decisions, fatigue, missed deadlines or appointment, inadequate time for rest or for the other aspects of life, and a sense of being overwhelmed by demands. The first step in proper time management is avoiding procrastination. Students should be encouraged to make daily lists of things they need to do, and to do first those things which they feel will be most difficult or which they are most likely to put off until later. Any effective time management program will also take into account the inevitable but unforeseen distractions and delays.

Progressive relaxation and visualization

Individuals who are trained in a means of conscious relaxation are more likely to handle stress effectively. Progressive relaxation and visualization are two techniques for relaxation. In progressive relaxation, the individual consciously increases and decreases tension in the muscles while sitting or lying down. This process can help quiet the mind and relieve physical tension. Visualization, or the use of guided imagery, is the creation of vivid mental pictures that will calm and focus the mind. This process is often used to help people with debilitating physical illnesses who, because of their condition, may not be able to perform more vigorous forms of relaxation. Visualization has been shown to enhance immune function and promote good health in the elderly.

Mediation and mindfulness

Two of the oldest and most proven methods of reducing stress are meditation and mindfulness. Meditation comes in a number of different forms, but is essentially the practice of calming the mind either by concentrating intently on one particular thing, or by trying to empty the mind of thought altogether. Many people have discovered meditation purely by chance and without any formal instruction. Mindfulness, like meditation, relies on the practice of measured breathing. However, mindfulness also entails attuning one's focus to the present moment. This simply means trying to be conscious of every experience you are undergoing, without judgment or the attempt to change anything. Mindfulness is designed to train the mind to deal with the present, rather than wasting time worrying about the past or future.

Biofeedback

Biofeedback is perhaps the most contemporary of the major methods of relaxation. In biofeedback, the individual obtains information about his or her physiology from some electronic monitoring device. Any change in the person's physiology will result in an immediate signal from the machine. Most of the time, the person receiving biofeedback can begin to assert some kind of control over his or her physiological responses to external events. Being trained in biofeedback is a three-part task. First, the individual develops an increased consciousness of a state or function of his or her body. Next, he or she develops some kind of control over this state or function. Finally, he or she is able to exhibit this control without the presence of the electronic machine. Biofeedback is considered successful when the subject is able to consistently produce alpha waves, a slower and more rhythmic brain wave.

Important terms

Alcoholic Brain Syndrome: A general term for a range of disorders due to the effects of alcohol on the brain—e.g., acute intoxication, pathological intoxication, withdrawal syndrome, delirium tremens, hallucinosis, amnesic syndrome, dementia, psychotic disorder.

Alcoholic Cardiomyopathy: A diffuse disorder of heart muscle seen in individuals with a history of hazardous consumption of alcohol, usually of at least 10 years' duration. Patients typically present with biventricular heart failure; common symptoms include shortness of breath on exertion and while recumbent, palpitations, ankle edema, and abdominal distension due to ascites. Disturbance of the cardiac rhythm is usual; atrial fibrillation is the most frequent arrhythmia.

Alcoholic Cirrhosis: A severe form of alcoholic liver disease, characterized by necrosis and permanent architectural distortion of the liver due to fibrous tissue formation and regeneratory nodules. This is a strictly histological definition, but diagnosis is often made on clinical grounds only. Alcoholic cirrhosis occurs mainly in the 40-60-year age group, after at least 10 years of hazardous drinking. Individuals show symptoms and signs of hepatic decompensation such as ascites, ankle edema, jaundice, bruising, gastrointestinal hemorrhage from esophageal varices, and confusion or stupor due to hepatic encephalopathy. Liver cancer is a late complication of cirrhosis in approximately 15% of cases.

Alcoholic Gastritis: Inflammation of the mucosal lining of the stomach caused by alcohol. It occurs typically after an alcoholic binge and is characterized by mucosal erosions, which may bleed. Symptoms include pain in the upper abdomen, and there may be gastric hemorrhage. Alcoholic gastritis is commonly accompanied by esophagitis. In most cases the condition is self-limiting and resolves with abstinence.

Alcoholic Hepatitis: A disorder of the liver characterized by liver cell necrosis and inflammation following chronic consumption of hazardous levels of alcohol. It is a well documented precursor of alcoholic cirrhosis, particularly in those whose alcohol intake remains high. Although the diagnosis is, strictly speaking, a histological one, it is often made on the basis of clinical and biochemical evidence, even if confirmation by biopsy is not possible. The diagnosis is suggested on clinical grounds by the presence of jaundice (which may be deep) and tender hepatomegaly, and sometimes ascites and hemorrhage.

Practice Test

Practice Questions

1. Which of the following are three common changes that can occur with drug abuse?
   a. Pharmacological
   b. Psychological
   c. Social
   d. All of the above

2. Which of the following is a drug that depresses brain activity?
   a. Ecstasy
   b. Tobacco
   c. Alcohol
   d. Cocaine

3. In synergism, one drug is used to _____ the performance of another drug.
   a. Depress
   b. Boost
   c. Stabilize
   d. Eliminate

4. What percentage of the alcohol consumed by a user is inactivated by the function of the liver?
   a. 10%
   b. 50%
   c. 100%
   d. 95%

5. Which of the following is a type of depressant that is used to promote sleep and affect memory?
   a. Nicotine
   b. Sedative
   c. Hypnotic
   d. Antihistamine

6. An inhalant that involves the use of a whipped cream dispenser would be what type of inhalant?
   a. Gas
   b. Volatile solvent
   c. Aerosol spray
   d. Nitrite

7. Why do inhalant abusers often inhale repeatedly over a long period of time instead of just once or twice?
   a. The abuser's judgment is impaired
   b. The high lasts for a short time
   c. Repeated inhaling is needed to achieve the high
   d. Inhalations must be done over a period of time for the high to be achieved

8. How are adolescent drug use and social maladjustment related?
   a. Drug use is a cause of maladjustment
   b. They are not related
   c. Maladjustment is a cause of drug use
   d. This is not determinable

9. What is the psychoactive ingredient in marijuana?
   a. Diamorphine
   b. Opioid
   c. Tetrahydrocannabinol
   d. Naltrexone

10. Monoamine oxidase inhibitors (MAOIs) are most often used to treat what type of problem?
   a. Depression
   b. Mild anxiety
   c. Psychosis
   d. Alcoholism

11. Nicotine increases the levels of which neurotransmitter?
   a. Histamine
   b. Serotonin
   c. Dopamine
   d. Epinephrine

12. Nicotine can
   a. Cause cancer
   b. Be toxic in high doses
   c. Cause lung cancer
   d. Increase an individual's risk of emphysema

13. When do "antagonistic interactions" occur?
    a. When one drug intensifies the effects of another
    b. When a particular drug produces negative effects, such as a "bad trip"
    c. When one drug eliminates the effects of another drug
    d. When the drug ingested does not produce the desired effect

14. The relationship between adolescent drug use and suicide is
    a. Causative
    b. Inconclusive
    c. Understood
    d. Not causative

15. The Drug Enforcement Agency (DEA) classifies heroin as a Schedule _____ drug.
    a. IV
    b. II
    c. III
    d. I

Answers and Explanations

1. D: (all of the above). There are many changes that can occur when an individual chooses to engage in drug abuse. The most obvious is pharmacological, which refers to the body chemistry changes that are caused as the drug alters physical performance and distorts reality. Psychological and social changes also occur in various ways, such as problems temporarily seeming insignificant, the abuser feeling more confident in a previously insecure ability, etc.

2. C: (alcohol). Depressants are among the most widely abused drugs, and alcohol is chief among them. Alcohol depresses brain activity and leaves the user with the sensation of feeling relaxed and sleepy; for this reason, it is often used as a stress management tool. However, alcohol consumption can also lead to dependence characterized by such things as cravings, loss of control, and physical dependence.

3. B: (boost). Drug abusers will sometimes combine the drugs they're taking in an attempt to alter the experiential outcome. Synergism is a type of drug interaction in which one drug's effect is enhanced by another drug's ingestion. In other cases, the abuser may combine one drug with another in an attempt to minimize the negative effects of one of them.

4. D: (95%). Metabolism is a way that the body can convert one substance into another. An enzyme in the human liver metabolizes most alcohol at an even pace, detoxifying it and removing it from the bloodstream. It can metabolize almost 95% of the alcohol consumed. As alcohol is consumed in larger amounts (and in less time), the alcohol that the liver cannot metabolize will spill over into the bloodstream.

5. C: (hypnotic). A hypnotic is a type of depressant that is used to promote sleep. Unlike a sedative, which is used to enhance relaxation and relieve anxiety, a hypnotic induces sleep and may also even cause amnesiac effects. The amnesiac effects are useful in medical treatments such as surgery so that a treatment can be completed without the patient having any memory of the procedure.

6. A: (gas). There are several types of inhalants. Volatile solvents are liquids that become gases when at room temperature, and gases are already in the gas state. Aerosol sprays are things like deodorant and hair sprays. Nitrites (found in some types of air fresheners) release inhalable substances when opened. Abuse of these various types of inhalants involves inhaling a substance through the lungs to create a temporary high.

7. B: (The high lasts for a short time). The high from inhalants can be achieved quite quickly. However, because the high generally lasts only a few minutes, the inhalant abuser often continues to use the inhalant over a long period of time (to maintain the high). Inhalants are quite dangerous because the level of toxic substance continues to increase in the abuser's system even after the initial high is achieved.

8. C: (Maladjustment is a cause of drug use). Adolescents turn to drug use for many reasons. These reasons can be anything from serious mental disorders and family dysfunction to the need to fit in with a peer group. The critical factor to remember, however, is that drug use is chosen for a reason, with that reason existing first and the drug abuse following secondarily from that reason.

9. C: (tetrahydrocannabinol). The psychoactive ingredient in marijuana is tetrahydrocannabinol (also known as THC). The results of smoking marijuana vary from person to person depending on such things as expectations, setting, and route of administration. Generally, the abuser experiences a sense of well-being, relaxation, and heightened sensory awareness as a result of the THC ingested.

10. A: (depression). MAOIs are commonly used second to tricyclic antidepressants because of their negative side effects, but MAOIs can be useful when other antidepressants have failed. MAOIs can have negative side effects with food and other drugs, including many stimulants that are abused (such as cocaine and ecstasy). This can create a very dangerous situation for those who are "self-medicating" in addition to taking an MAOI.

11. C: (dopamine). Nicotine increases the levels of dopamine, a neurotransmitter that affects the parts of the brain that control pleasure. The continued use of nicotine over time can lead to changes in the brain that result in addiction. When the long-term user attempts to quit, these brain changes can cause the user to crave nicotine and experience negative side effects from the nicotine no longer being present.

12. B: (be toxic in high doses). Although nicotine can be toxic in high doses, it does not cause the many health issues that tobacco is responsible for. Tobacco smoke is a mix of many potentially dangerous substances, including some that are known carcinogens. Nicotine itself can negatively affect heart rate, blood pressure, and other body processes. Nicotine is of course addictive, but that is not the only negative aspect of tobacco abuse.

13. C: (when one drug eliminates the effects of another drug). Unlike synergism (in which the ingestion of one drug enhances the performance of another drug), antagonistic interactions involve removing the effects of a drug. Abusers will sometimes do this in an attempt to reduce or eliminate the negative effects of the initial drug they take. For example, if one drug produces drowsiness as a side effect, a second drug may be ingested to counter that response.

14. D: (not causative). Drugs are abused by teens, just as with other populations, for a variety of reasons. Because drugs are often used by suicidal teens and because adolescents are at a higher risk for suicide, the two are often linked together. However, there is no cause-and-effect correlation between drug use and adolescent suicide at this time.

15. D: (I). Drugs placed in Schedule I have the highest abuse potential. Heroin is one of the most abused drugs in the United States. It is not approved for clinical use and has a very high mortality rate. Because of its high degree of abuse as well as its high level of health risk, heroin is considered a Schedule I drug.

Secret Key #1 - Time is Your Greatest Enemy

Pace Yourself

Wear a watch. At the beginning of the test, check the time (or start a chronometer on your watch to count the minutes), and check the time after every few questions to make sure you are "on schedule."

If you are forced to speed up, do it efficiently. Usually one or more answer choices can be eliminated without too much difficulty. Above all, don't panic. Don't speed up and just begin guessing at random choices. By pacing yourself, and continually monitoring your progress against your watch, you will always know exactly how far ahead or behind you are with your available time. If you find that you are one minute behind on the test, don't skip one question without spending any time on it, just to catch back up. Take 15 fewer seconds on the next four questions, and after four questions you'll have caught back up. Once you catch back up, you can continue working each problem at your normal pace.

Furthermore, don't dwell on the problems that you were rushed on. If a problem was taking up too much time and you made a hurried guess, it must be difficult. The difficult questions are the ones you are most likely to miss anyway, so it isn't a big loss. It is better to end with more time than you need than to run out of time.

Lastly, sometimes it is beneficial to slow down if you are constantly getting ahead of time. You are always more likely to catch a careless mistake by working more slowly than quickly, and among very high-scoring test takers (those who are likely to have lots of time left over), careless errors affect the score more than mastery of material.

Secret Key #2 - Guessing is not Guesswork

You probably know that guessing is a good idea - unlike other standardized tests, there is no penalty for getting a wrong answer. Even if you have no idea about a question, you still have a 20-25% chance of getting it right.

Most test takers do not understand the impact that proper guessing can have on their score. Unless you score extremely high, guessing will significantly contribute to your final score.

Monkeys Take the Test

What most test takers don't realize is that to insure that 20-25% chance, you have to guess randomly. If you put 20 monkeys in a room to take this test, assuming they answered once per question and behaved themselves, on average they would get 20-25% of the questions correct. Put 20 test takers in the room, and the average will be much lower among guessed questions. Why?

1. The test writers intentionally write deceptive answer choices that "look" right. A test taker has no idea about a question, so picks the "best looking" answer, which is often wrong. The monkey has no idea what looks good and what doesn't, so will consistently be lucky about 20-25% of the time.
2. Test takers will eliminate answer choices from the guessing pool based on a hunch or intuition. Simple but correct answers often get excluded, leaving a 0% chance of being correct. The monkey has no clue, and often gets lucky with the best choice.

This is why the process of elimination endorsed by most test courses is flawed and detrimental to your performance- test takers don't guess, they make an ignorant stab in the dark that is usually worse than random.

$5 Challenge

Let me introduce one of the most valuable ideas of this course- the $5 challenge:

You only mark your "best guess" if you are willing to bet $5 on it.

You only eliminate choices from guessing if you are willing to bet $5 on it.

Why $5? Five dollars is an amount of money that is small yet not insignificant, and can really add up fast (20 questions could cost you $100). Likewise, each answer choice on one question of the test will have a small impact on your overall score, but it can really add up to a lot of points in the end.

The process of elimination IS valuable. The following shows your chance of guessing it right:

If you eliminate wrong answer choices until only this many remain:	1	2	3
Chance of getting it correct:	100%	50%	33%

However, if you accidentally eliminate the right answer or go on a hunch for an incorrect answer, your chances drop dramatically: to 0%. By guessing among all the answer choices, you are GUARANTEED to have a shot at the right answer.

That's why the $5 test is so valuable- if you give up the advantage and safety of a pure guess, it had better be worth the risk.

What we still haven't covered is how to be sure that whatever guess you make is truly random. Here's the easiest way:

Always pick the first answer choice among those remaining.

Such a technique means that you have decided, **before you see a single test question**, exactly how you are going to guess- and since the order of choices tells you nothing about which one is correct, this guessing technique is perfectly random.

This section is not meant to scare you away from making educated guesses or eliminating choices- you just need to define when a choice is worth eliminating. The $5 test, along with a pre-defined random guessing strategy, is the best way to make sure you reap all of the benefits of guessing.

Secret Key #3 - Practice Smarter, Not Harder

Many test takers delay the test preparation process because they dread the awful amounts of practice time they think necessary to succeed on the test. We have refined an effective method that will take you only a fraction of the time.

There are a number of "obstacles" in your way to succeed. Among these are answering questions, finishing in time, and mastering test-taking strategies. All must be executed on the day of the test at peak performance, or your score will suffer. The test is a mental marathon that has a large impact on your future.

Just like a marathon runner, it is important to work your way up to the full challenge. So first you just worry about questions, and then time, and finally strategy:

Success Strategy

1. Find a good source for practice tests.
2. If you are willing to make a larger time investment, consider using more than

one study guide- often the different approaches of multiple authors will help you "get" difficult concepts.

3. Take a practice test with no time constraints, with all study helps "open book." Take your time with questions and focus on applying strategies.

4. Take a practice test with time constraints, with all guides "open book."

5. Take a final practice test with no open material and time limits

If you have time to take more practice tests, just repeat step 5. By gradually exposing yourself to the full rigors of the test environment, you will condition your mind to the stress of test day and maximize your success.

Secret Key #4 - Prepare, Don't Procrastinate

Let me state an obvious fact: if you take the test three times, you will get three different scores. This is due to the way you feel on test day, the level of preparedness you have, and, despite the test writers' claims to the contrary, some tests WILL be easier for you than others.

Since your future depends so much on your score, you should maximize your chances of success. In order to maximize the likelihood of success, you've got to prepare in advance. This means taking practice tests and spending time learning the information and test taking strategies you will need to succeed.

Never take the test as a "practice" test, expecting that you can just take it again if you need to. Feel free to take sample tests on your own, but when you go to take the official test, be prepared, be focused, and do your best the first time!

Secret Key #5 - Test Yourself

Everyone knows that time is money. There is no need to spend too much of your time or too little of your time preparing for the test. You should only spend as much of your precious time preparing as is necessary for you to get the score you need.

Once you have taken a practice test under real conditions of time constraints, then you will know if you are ready for the test or not.

If you have scored extremely high the first time that you take the practice test, then there is not much point in spending countless hours studying. You are already there.

Benchmark your abilities by retaking practice tests and seeing how much you have improved. Once you score high enough to guarantee success, then you are ready.

If you have scored well below where you need, then knuckle down and begin studying in earnest. Check your improvement regularly through the use of practice tests under real conditions. Above all, don't worry, panic, or give up. The key is perseverance!

Then, when you go to take the test, remain confident and remember how well you did on the practice tests. If you can score high enough on a practice test, then you can do the same on the real thing.

General Strategies

The most important thing you can do is to ignore your fears and jump into the test immediately- do not be overwhelmed by any strange-sounding terms. You have to jump into the test like jumping into a pool- all at once is the easiest way.

Make Predictions

As you read and understand the question, try to guess what the answer will be. Remember that several of the answer choices are wrong, and once you begin reading them, your mind will immediately become cluttered with answer choices designed to throw you off. Your mind is typically the most focused immediately after you have read the question and digested its contents. If you can, try to predict what the correct answer will be. You may be surprised at what you can predict.

Quickly scan the choices and see if your prediction is in the listed answer choices. If it is, then you can be quite confident that you have the right answer. It still won't hurt to check the other answer choices, but most of the time, you've got it!

Answer the Question

It may seem obvious to only pick answer choices that answer the question, but the test writers can create some excellent answer choices that are wrong. Don't pick an answer just because it sounds right, or you believe it to be true. It MUST answer the question. Once you've made your selection, always go back and check it against the question and make sure that you didn't misread the question, and the answer choice does answer the question posed.

Benchmark

After you read the first answer choice, decide if you think it sounds correct or not. If it doesn't, move on to the next answer choice. If it does, mentally mark that answer choice. This doesn't mean that you've definitely selected it as your answer choice, it

- 167 -

just means that it's the best you've seen thus far. Go ahead and read the next choice. If the next choice is worse than the one you've already selected, keep going to the next answer choice. If the next choice is better than the choice you've already selected, mentally mark the new answer choice as your best guess.

The first answer choice that you select becomes your standard. Every other answer choice must be benchmarked against that standard. That choice is correct until proven otherwise by another answer choice beating it out. Once you've decided that no other answer choice seems as good, do one final check to ensure that your answer choice answers the question posed.

Valid Information

Don't discount any of the information provided in the question. Every piece of information may be necessary to determine the correct answer. None of the information in the question is there to throw you off (while the answer choices will certainly have information to throw you off). If two seemingly unrelated topics are discussed, don't ignore either. You can be confident there is a relationship, or it wouldn't be included in the question, and you are probably going to have to determine what is that relationship to find the answer.

Avoid "Fact Traps"

Don't get distracted by a choice that is factually true. Your search is for the answer that answers the question. Stay focused and don't fall for an answer that is true but incorrect. Always go back to the question and make sure you're choosing an answer that actually answers the question and is not just a true statement. An answer can be factually correct, but it MUST answer the question asked. Additionally, two answers can both be seemingly correct, so be sure to read all of the answer choices, and make sure that you get the one that BEST answers the question.

Milk the Question

Some of the questions may throw you completely off. They might deal with a subject you have not been exposed to, or one that you haven't reviewed in years. While your lack of knowledge about the subject will be a hindrance, the question itself can give you many clues that will help you find the correct answer. Read the question carefully and look for clues. Watch particularly for adjectives and nouns describing difficult terms or words that you don't recognize. Regardless of if you completely understand a word or not, replacing it with a synonym either provided or one you more familiar with may help you to understand what the questions are asking. Rather than wracking your mind about specific detailed information concerning a difficult term or word, try to use mental substitutes that are easier to understand.

The Trap of Familiarity

Don't just choose a word because you recognize it. On difficult questions, you may not recognize a number of words in the answer choices. The test writers don't put "make-believe" words on the test; so don't think that just because you only recognize all the words in one answer choice means that answer choice must be correct. If you only recognize words in one answer choice, then focus on that one. Is it correct? Try your best to determine if it is correct. If it is, that is great, but if it doesn't, eliminate it. Each word and answer choice you eliminate increases your chances of getting the question correct, even if you then have to guess among the unfamiliar choices.

Eliminate Answers

Eliminate choices as soon as you realize they are wrong. But be careful! Make sure you consider all of the possible answer choices. Just because one appears right, doesn't mean that the next one won't be even better! The test writers will usually put more than one good answer choice for every question, so read all of them. Don't worry if you are stuck between two that seem right. By getting down to just two remaining possible choices, your odds are now 50/50. Rather than wasting too much time, play the odds. You are guessing, but guessing wisely, because you've been able to knock out some of the answer choices that you know are wrong. If you are eliminating choices and realize that the last answer choice you are left with is also obviously wrong, don't panic. Start over and consider each choice again. There may easily be something that you missed the first time and will realize on the second pass.

Tough Questions

If you are stumped on a problem or it appears too hard or too difficult, don't waste time. Move on! Remember though, if you can quickly check for obviously incorrect answer choices, your chances of guessing correctly are greatly improved. Before you completely give up, at least try to knock out a couple of possible answers. Eliminate what you can and then guess at the remaining answer choices before moving on.

Brainstorm

If you get stuck on a difficult question, spend a few seconds quickly brainstorming. Run through the complete list of possible answer choices. Look at each choice and ask yourself, "Could this answer the question satisfactorily?" Go through each answer choice and consider it independently of the other. By systematically going through all possibilities, you may find something that you would otherwise overlook. Remember that when you get stuck, it's important to try to keep moving.

Read Carefully

Understand the problem. Read the question and answer choices carefully. Don't miss the question because you misread the terms. You have plenty of time to read each question thoroughly and make sure you understand what is being asked. Yet a happy medium must be attained, so don't waste too much time. You must read carefully, but efficiently.

Face Value

When in doubt, use common sense. Always accept the situation in the problem at face value. Don't read too much into it. These problems will not require you to make huge leaps of logic. The test writers aren't trying to throw you off with a cheap trick. If you have to go beyond creativity and make a leap of logic in order to have an answer choice answer the question, then you should look at the other answer choices. Don't overcomplicate the problem by creating theoretical relationships or explanations that will warp time or space. These are normal problems rooted in reality. It's just that the applicable relationship or explanation may not be readily apparent and you have to figure things out. Use your common sense to interpret anything that isn't clear.

Prefixes

If you're having trouble with a word in the question or answer choices, try dissecting it. Take advantage of every clue that the word might include. Prefixes and suffixes can be a huge help. Usually they allow you to determine a basic meaning. Pre- means before, post- means after, pro - is positive, de- is negative. From these prefixes and suffixes, you can get an idea of the general meaning of the word and try to put it into context. Beware though of any traps. Just because con is the opposite of pro, doesn't necessarily mean congress is the opposite of progress!

Hedge Phrases

Watch out for critical "hedge" phrases, such as likely, may, can, will often, sometimes, often, almost, mostly, usually, generally, rarely, sometimes. Question writers insert these hedge phrases to cover every possibility. Often an answer choice will be wrong simply because it leaves no room for exception. Avoid answer choices that have definitive words like "exactly," and "always".

Switchback Words

Stay alert for "switchbacks". These are the words and phrases frequently used to alert you to shifts in thought. The most common switchback word is "but". Others include although, however, nevertheless, on the other hand, even though, while, in spite of, despite, regardless of.

New Information

Correct answer choices will rarely have completely new information included. Answer choices typically are straightforward reflections of the material asked about and will directly relate to the question. If a new piece of information is included in an answer choice that doesn't even seem to relate to the topic being asked about, then that answer choice is likely incorrect. All of the information needed to answer the question is usually provided for you, and so you should not have to make guesses that are unsupported or choose answer choices that require unknown information that cannot be reasoned on its own.

Time Management

On technical questions, don't get lost on the technical terms. Don't spend too much time on any one question. If you don't know what a term means, then since you don't have a dictionary, odds are you aren't going to get much further. You should immediately recognize terms as whether or not you know them. If you don't, work with the other clues that you have, the other answer choices and terms provided, but don't waste too much time trying to figure out a difficult term.

Contextual Clues

Look for contextual clues. An answer can be right but not correct. The contextual clues will help you find the answer that is most right and is correct. Understand the context in which a phrase or statement is made. This will help you make important distinctions.

Don't Panic

Panicking will not answer any questions for you. Therefore, it isn't helpful. When you first see the question, if your mind goes blank, take a deep breath. Force yourself to mechanically go through the steps of solving the problem and using the strategies you've learned.

Pace Yourself

Don't get clock fever. It's easy to be overwhelmed when you're looking at a page full of questions, your mind is full of random thoughts and feeling confused, and the clock is ticking down faster than you would like. Calm down and maintain the pace that you have set for yourself. As long as you are on track by monitoring your pace, you are guaranteed to have enough time for yourself. When you get to the last few minutes of the test, it may seem like you won't have enough time left, but if you only have as many questions as you should have left at that point, then you're right on track!

Answer Selection

The best way to pick an answer choice is to eliminate all of those that are wrong, until only one is left and confirm that is the correct answer. Sometimes though, an answer choice may immediately look right. Be careful! Take a second to make sure that the other choices are not equally obvious. Don't make a hasty mistake. There are only two times that you should stop before checking other answers. First is when you are positive that the answer choice you have selected is correct. Second is when time is almost out and you have to make a quick guess!

Check Your Work

Since you will probably not know every term listed and the answer to every question, it is important that you get credit for the ones that you do know. Don't miss any questions through careless mistakes. If at all possible, try to take a second to look back over your answer selection and make sure you've selected the correct answer choice and haven't made a costly careless mistake (such as marking an answer choice that you didn't mean to mark). This quick double check should more than pay for itself in caught mistakes for the time it costs.

Beware of Directly Quoted Answers

Sometimes an answer choice will repeat word for word a portion of the question or reference section. However, beware of such exact duplication – it may be a trap! More than likely, the correct choice will paraphrase or summarize a point, rather than being exactly the same wording.

Slang

Scientific sounding answers are better than slang ones. An answer choice that begins "To compare the outcomes..." is much more likely to be correct than one that begins "Because some people insisted..."

Extreme Statements

Avoid wild answers that throw out highly controversial ideas that are proclaimed as established fact. An answer choice that states the "process should be used in certain situations, if..." is much more likely to be correct than one that states the "process should be discontinued completely." The first is a calm rational statement and doesn't even make a definitive, uncompromising stance, using a hedge word "if" to provide wiggle room, whereas the second choice is a radical idea and far more extreme.

Answer Choice Families

When you have two or more answer choices that are direct opposites or parallels, one of them is usually the correct answer. For instance, if one answer choice states "x increases" and another answer choice states "x decreases" or "y increases," then those two or three answer choices are very similar in construction and fall into the same family of answer choices. A family of answer choices is when two or three answer choices are very similar in construction, and yet often have a directly opposite meaning. Usually the correct answer choice will be in that family of answer choices. The "odd man out" or answer choice that doesn't seem to fit the parallel construction of the other answer choices is more likely to be incorrect.